Getting in Touch with God

JIM BURNS

HARVEST HOUSE PUBLISHERS
Eugene, Oregon 97402

GETTING IN TOUCH WITH GOD

Copyright © 1986 by Harvest House Publishers
Eugene, Oregon 97402

Library of Congress Catalog Card Number 86-080714
ISBN 0-89081-520-8

Printed in the United States of America.

To my daughter, Christy Meredith Burns:

You have brought me a deeper love and serendipity than I ever imagined possible. Your enthusiasm, spontaneity, and zeal for life daily provide me with a fresh appreciation of God's goodness and faithfulness.
I can never adequately express my gratitude to God for your coming into our life.
You are loved. . .

Agape,
Dad

CONTENTS

7. OBEDIENCE

8. ATTITUDE

9. COMMITMENT

Getting in Touch with God

CELEBRATE LIFE

DAY 1

Celebrate This Heartbeat

Brothers, I do not consider myself yet to have taken hold of it. But one thing I do: Forgetting what was behind and straining toward what is ahead, I press on toward the goal to win the prize for which God has called me heavenward in Christ Jesus.

—Philippians 3:13,14

I like what the psalmist wrote so long ago: "This is the day the Lord has made; let us rejoice and be glad in it" (Psalm 118:24). Each day you live is a gift from God. There will never be another today—so make the most of today. Live life to the fullest. It seems like the majority of people today are paralyzed by their past and are always looking for a brighter tomorrow while not making the most of today. I think the words of this contemporary Christian song make a lot of sense.

I'm gonna celebrate this heartbeat
'Cause it just might be my last.

Every day is a gift from the Lord on high,
And they all go by so fast.
So many people drifting in a dream,
I only want to live the real thing.
I'm gonna celebrate this heartbeat
And keep movin' on,
Look toward tomorrow 'cause the past is
    gone.

If I laugh, it's no crime—
I've got great news on my mind.
It's a hope that never fades away.
Now I don't understand
All the mysteries of the Master plan,
But I'm sure the Master does,
So that's okay.*

Because God has promised to take care of your tomorrow, you can celebrate life to the fullest today.

CHALLENGE

Paul said, "Brothers, I do not consider myself yet to have taken hold of it. But one thing I do: Forgetting what is behind and straining toward what is ahead, I press on toward the goal to win the prize for which God has called me heavenward in Christ Jesus" (Philippians 3:13,14). How does this verse apply to you? What can you do to make each day more of a celebration in your life?

* Randy Stonehill, *Celebrate This Heartbeat* (Waco: Word Records, Inc., 1984).

DAY 2

Grasp the Hour

*Whatever you do, whether in word or deed, do
it all in the name of the Lord Jesus, giving thanks
to God the Father through him.*
                                    —Colossians 3:17

Life is a celebration. Don't postpone it. Grasp the
hour! Today is the first day of the rest of your life.
Here is a list of possibilities to make your day a
brighter day.

- Seek out a forgotten friend.
- Write a love letter.
- Share a treasure.
- Encourage someone with a kind word.
- Keep a promise.
- Give to a needy cause.
- Forgive an enemy.
- Listen.
- Apologize if you were wrong.
- Try to understand.

- Read your Bible.
- Pray for your family.
- Examine your demands on others.
- Appreciate a friend.
- Be kind, be gentle.
- Laugh a little.
- Laugh a little more.
- Take pleasure in the beauty and wonder of the earth.*

CHALLENGE

Don't forget to celebrate life today. You'll never have another day like today. Don't go on until you make a decision to do at least two of these suggestions *today!*

---

* Idea taken from *Crossroads* newsletter of the First Christian Church; June 11, 1978.

DAY 3

Enjoy Life!

Do not be anxious about anything, but in every-thing, by prayer and petition, with thanksgiving, present your requests to God. And the peace of God, which transcends all understanding, will guard your hearts and your minds in Christ Jesus.
—Philippians 4:6,7

Sometimes I work too hard and take life too seriously. Last week I noticed flowers in my backyard in bloom, and I had missed the process of blooming. Life is too short. Sometimes we need to sit back and enjoy God's gift to us.

Brother Jeremiah was at the end of his life when he reflected on his many years of Christian service. I keep close to my heart these words he wrote:

If I had my life to live over again, I'd try
to make more mistakes next time. I
would relax. I would limber up. I would
be sillier than I have been this trip. I
know of very few things I would take

15

seriously. I would take more trips. I would climb more mountains, swim more rivers, and watch more sunsets. I would do more walking and looking. I would eat more ice cream and less beans. I would have more actual troubles and fewer imaginary ones.

You see, I am one of those people who live prophylactically and sensibly and sanely, hour after hour, day after day. Oh, I've had my moments, and if I had it to do over again, I'd have more of them. In fact, I'd try to have nothing else. Just moments, one after another, instead of living so many years ahead each day. I have been one of those people who never go anywhere without a thermometer, a hot water bottle, a gargle, a raincoat, aspirin, and a parachute. If I had it to do over again, I would go places, do things, and travel lighter than I have.

If I had my life to live over, I would start barefooted earlier in the spring and stay that way later in the fall. I would play more. I would ride on more merry-go-rounds. I'd pick more daisies.*

---

* Ted W. Engstrom, *The Pursuit of Excellence* (Grand Rapids: Zondervan, 1982), p. 90. Used by permission.

CHALLENGE

Have you taken time this week to stop and view a sunset or go on an adventure? Maybe it's time to get off the rat race and experience God's gift of life. What crazy, almost silly event can you do this week? What's keeping you from doing it? Don't wait! Now is the time to live life to the fullest.

DAY 4

Life Is Too Short For...

Do not worry about tomorrow, for tomorrow will worry about itself. Each day has enough trouble of its own.

—Matthew 6:34

One day when I was caught up in the tyranny of the urgent, my friend Bill McNabb sent me some thoughts entitled "Things That Life Is Too Short For." His thoughts forced me to take a look at my own life and reevaluate my priorities. Perhaps you need a dose of reality today. I'll share these special thoughts with you.

- Life is too short to nurse grudges or hurt feelings.
- It's too short to worry about getting ready for Christmas. Just let Christmas come.
- It's too short to keep all your floors shiny.

- It's too short to let a day pass without hugging your loved ones.
- It's too short not to take a nap when you need one.
- It's too short to put off Bible study.
- It's too short to give importance to whether the towels match the bathroom.
- It's too short to miss the call to worship on a Sunday morning.
- It's too short to stay indoors on a crisp fall Saturday.
- It's too short to read all the junk mail.
- It's too short not to call or write your parents (or children) regularly.
- It's too short to work at a job you hate.
- It's too short not to stop and talk to children.
- It's too short to forget to pray.
- It's too short to put off improving our relationships with people that we love.
- Life is just too short. Way too short to settle for mediocrity!

CHALLENGE

Do you tend to get caught up in things that seem important but in reality keep you from experiencing all that God has in store for you? If you do, then reread today's thought and make a decision to enjoy your life today!

DAY 5

Making the Most
of Today

*This is the day the Lord has made; let us
rejoice and be glad in it.*

—Psalm 118:24

Today you were handed from God 24 hours to
live life to the fullest. That's 1440 minutes or
86,400 seconds. Sometimes we get so busy and distracted we miss the fact that each rising sun brings
new opportunities and adventures on this planet
we call Earth. God gives us one new day at a time
so that we aren't distracted by the future or paralyzed by the past. Today is the first day of the rest
of your life.

Make the most of today. Enjoy God's gift to you.
You can accomplish a great deal with each 1440
minutes in a day. Today stop and take advantage of
all that God has provided for you. Here are a few
suggestions:

- Tell someone you love him.
- Write a kind note to a friend.
- Stop and enjoy the sunset.
- Take 20 minutes of the 1440 you have today and talk to God.
- Memorize this verse:

"This is the day the Lord has made; let us rejoice and be glad in it."

—Psalm 118:24

CHALLENGE

Take a moment to thank God for His gift of time, and plot out a plan to make the most of the day. Say along with Dag Hammarskjold:

For all that has been—Thanks.
To all that shall be—Yes!

DAY 6

Your Use of Time

Thou hast made the moon to mark the seasons;
the sun knows its time for setting.
                              —Psalm 104:19 RSV

The greatest commodity you have at your fingertips is *time*. Everyone has the same amount of time to use or waste today. The happiness in your life depends on how you use your time. Periodically I need to take an evaluation of how I am using my time. This little paragraph helps me keep perspective:

Take time to THINK—it is the source of
    power.
Take time to PLAY—it is the secret of
    perpetual youth.
Take time to be FRIENDLY—it is the
    road to happiness.
Take time to LOVE—it is a God-given
    privilege.

Take time to READ—it is a fountain of
wisdom.
Take time to PRAY—it is the greatest
power on earth.
Take time to LAUGH—it is the music of
the soul.
Take time to GIVE—it is too short a day
to be selfish.
Take time to WORK—it is the price of
success.

CHALLENGE

How do your time commitments measure up to
the paragraph above? Today take a few minutes to
evaluate how you spend your time. These minutes
just might be the wisest investment of time you've
made in a long time.

DAY 7

What Can We Learn from Death?

Just as man is destined to die once, and after that to face judgment, so Christ was sacrificed once to take away the sins of many people; and he will appear a second time, not to bear sin, but to bring salvation to those who are waiting for him.

—Hebrews 9:27,28

No one likes to talk or think about his death or the death of his loved ones. However, there are certain facts we can learn from death.

1. We will all die.
2. Life is short, so we should make the most of each day.
3. Celebrate life daily. Live now—don't wait.
4. Walk with God the Creator and Sustainer of life.

I like what Leo Buscaglia says about death and life:

> Death teaches us—if we want to hear— that the time is now. The time is now to pick up a telephone and call the person that you love. Death teaches us the joy of the moment. It teaches us we don't have forever. It teaches us that nothing is permanent. It teaches us to let go, there's nothing you can hang on to. And it tells us to give up expectations and let tomorrow tell its own story, because nobody knows if they'll get home tonight. To me that's a tremendous challenge. Death says "live now." Let's tell the children that.*

CHALLENGE

What actions or steps can you take in your life today to insure that you live life to the fullest, before it's too late?

---

* Leo Buscaglia, *Living, Loving and Learning* (New York: Random House, 1982), p. 153.

2 *JESUS IS LORD*

DAY 1

The Uniqueness of Christ

Jesus answered, "I am the way and the truth and the life. No one comes to the Father except through me."

—John 14:6

No person who has ever walked this earth even comes close to comparison when placed up against Jesus Christ. He is unique. He is incomparable. He is our Lord.

Here is what one unknown person wrote about Him years ago.

More than 1900 years ago there was a Man born contrary to the laws of life. This Man lived in poverty and was reared in obscurity. He did not travel extensively. Only once did He cross the boundary of the country in which He lived; that was during His exile in childhood. He possessed neither wealth nor influence.

His relatives were inconspicuous and had neither training nor formal education.

In infancy He startled a king; in childhood He puzzled doctors; in manhood He ruled the course of nature, walked upon the billows as if pavements, and hushed the sea to sleep. He healed the multitudes without medicine and made no charge for His service.

He never wrote a book, yet all the libraries of the country could not hold the books that have been written about Him. He never wrote a song, and yet He has furnished the theme for more songs than all the songwriters combined. He never founded a college, but all the schools put together cannot boast of having as many students. He never marshaled an army, nor drafted a soldier, nor fired a gun; and yet no leader ever had more volunteers who have, under his orders, made more rebels stack arms and surrender without a shot fired. He never practiced medicine, and yet He has healed more broken hearts than all the doctors far and near.

Every seventh day the wheels of commerce cease their turning as multitudes wend their way to worshiping assemblies to pay homage and respect to Him. The names of the past proud statesmen of Greece and Rome have come and gone, but the name of this Man abounds more and more. Though time has spread 1900 years between the people of this generation and the scene of His crucifixion, yet He still lives. Herod could not destroy Him and the grave could not hold Him.

He stands forth upon the highest pinnacle of heavenly glory, proclaimed of God, acknowledged by angels, adored by saints, and feared by devils as the living, personal Christ, our Lord and Savior.

—Anonymous

CHALLENGE

Are you in love with the God/man Jesus Christ? Have you put your faith and trust in Him? He is unique and incomparable because He is your God and Savior.

DAY 2

Open Your Heart
to Jesus

*Here I am! I stand at the door and knock. If
anyone hears my voice and opens the door, I will
come in and eat with him, and he with me.*
—Revelation 3:20

Billy Graham once said, "I have searched the
world over in my travels for contented and happy
men. I have found such men only where Christ has
been personally and decisively received. There is
only one permanent way to have peace of soul that
wells up in joy, contentment, and happiness, and
that is by repentance of sin and personal faith in
Jesus Christ as Savior."

Throughout the centuries Jesus Christ continues
to heal broken hearts and broken spirits. All over
the world today He is placing hope into shattered
lives and peace into troubled souls. When you get
in touch with Jesus Christ, one thing is guaranteed:
You will never remain the same.

I love the old Russian proverb that says *"He who has this disease called Jesus Christ will never be cured."*

CHALLENGE

Jesus doesn't force His way into your heart. He knocks, and you must open the door. If you need to give Him more room in your life, open wide the door and invite Him to take over the lordship of your life today.

DAY 3

The Resurrection of Jesus Christ

If Christ has not been raised, your faith is futile; you are still in your sins.
—1 Corinthians 15:17

The resurrection of Jesus Christ from the dead is the cornerstone of our Christian faith. If Christ did not rise from the dead, your faith is in vain. But you can be assured that the good news is true. Jesus Christ "was buried [and] was raised on the third day according to the Scriptures" (1 Corinthians 15:4).

Throughout the ages skeptics have tried to disprove the resurrection experience, but it stands the test of time. Here are six proofs that Jesus actually rose from the dead.

First Proof: The resurrection was foretold by Jesus Christ, the Son of God.

"From that time on Jesus began to explain to his disciples that he must go to Jerusalem and suffer many things at the hands of the elders, chief priests and teachers of the law, and that he must be killed and on the third day be raised to life" (Matthew 16:21).

Second Proof: The resurrection is the only reasonable explanation for His empty tomb.

"Joseph bought some linen cloth, took down the body, wrapped it in the linen, and placed it in a tomb cut out of rock. Then he rolled a stone against the entrance of the tomb" (Mark 15:46).

Third Proof: The resurrection is the only reasonable explanation for the appearance of Jesus Christ to His disciples.

"He was buried...was raised on the third day according to the Scriptures, and...appeared to Peter, and then to the Twelve. After that, he appeared to more than five hundred of the brothers at the same time, most of whom are still living, though some have fallen asleep. Then he appeared to...me also, as to one abnormally born"(1 Corinthians 15:4-8).

Fourth Proof: The resurrection is the only reasonable explanation for the beginning of the Christian church.

"This man was handed over to you by God's set purpose and foreknowledge;

and you, with the help of wicked men, put him to death by nailing him to the cross. But God raised him from the dead, freeing him from the agony of death, because it was impossible for death to keep its hold on him" (Acts 2:23,24).

Fifth Proof: The resurrection is the only reasonable explanation for the transformation of the disciples.

The disciples went into hiding in an upper room "for fear of the Jews." After seeing and talking with Jesus for approximately six weeks, they went out to "turn the world upside down," fearlessly proclaiming Jesus Christ (Acts 8:4; 17:6; 3:12-26; 4:1-33).

Sixth Proof: The witness of the apostle Paul, and the transformation of his life, can be reasonably explained only because of the resurrection of Christ.

"Saul grew more and more powerful and baffled the Jews living in Damascus by proving that Jesus is the Christ" (Acts 9:22).

CHALLENGE

Are you experiencing the resurrection power of Jesus in your life right now? The miracle of the resurrection can occur daily in your life as well.

DAY 4

The Incarnation

The Word became flesh and lived for a while
among us. We have seen his glory, the glory of
the one and only Son, who came from the Father,
full of grace and truth.

—John 1:14

How do you package love? God used a stable and
straw on the eve of Christ's birth. The incarnation
means that Jesus Christ is God in the flesh. Paul
put it this way: "He is the visible expression of
the invisible God." I heard a story as a child
that helped me understand this concept. It's about
ants.

> Once upon a time there was a colony of
> ants who were busy doing whatever ants
> do with their lives. God wanted to tell the
> ants of His love for them and His eternal
> home prepared for them. What was the
> very best way for God to communicate to
> those ants? The only possible way to

speak to the ants was to become an ant and speak their language. So He did, and they believed.

The only way for us to fully recognize God was for God to come to earth in the form of a man to identify with the world. Jesus was fully God and fully man; He knows what you are going through because He lived on this earth and completely identified with humankind. Hebrews 2:17,18 helps us understand the incarnation of Jesus and how He relates to our life:

> For this reason he had to be made like his brothers in every way, in order that he might become a merciful and faithful high priest in service to God, and that he might make atonement for the sins of the people. Because he himself suffered when he was tempted, he is able to help those who are being tempted.

CHALLENGE

Jesus Christ is God. When you give your life to Jesus you are getting in touch with the Creator, Savior, and Sustainer of the universe.

Jesus Is Lord

Let all Israel be assured of this: God has made this Jesus, whom you crucified, both Lord and Christ.

—Acts 2:36

In the Gospels there is a graphic story of Jesus standing before Pontius Pilate, the Roman governor. At one point in the story Pilate offers to release a prisoner to the Jews. He offers either Jesus or Barabbas (who was a troublemaker and murderer). The crowd asks for Barabbas to be freed. Pilate doesn't know what to do. He asks the crowd, "What shall I do with the man Jesus?" They cry, "Crucify him!"

The question Pilate asked, "What will you do with Jesus?" is still the important question of the day. When people today are confronted with Christ, they basically have four options. Which option have you chosen?

1. *Reject Him.* Turn your back on Jesus and live your life without Him.

2. *Ignore Him.* Choose to be an Easter and Christmas Christian. Acknowledge His deity but keep Him out of the practical daily activities of your life.

3. *Appease Him.* There are the people who go through the motions of Christianity but still keep the lordship of Christ at a distance.

4. *Obey Him.* If you obey Him you are choosing to make Him Lord of your life. You are no longer in control, He is. You choose to obey His will and His Word.

What will you do with the claims of Christ in your life? If you fall into one of the categories besides obedience, then perhaps it's time to make Him the Lord of your life. If you believe He is Christ the Savior, then your only true option is to make Him Christ the Lord also!

CHALLENGE

The first creed of the early Christians was "Jesus is Lord." Can you say that the creed of the early Christians is also your creed? Are you living your life as if Jesus is your Lord?

DAY 6

Lord, Liar, or Lunatic?

I and the Father are one.

—John 10:30

On a recent airplane trip a woman saw me reading the Bible. She was curious and asked me pointblank if I really believed that Jesus Christ was the Son of God. I replied that I indeed believed that Jesus is the Christ, the Son of the living God. Then she asked, "Isn't it difficult for you to intellectually believe such a preposterous statement as Jesus being God's only Son?"

My reply went something like this: "In the Bible Jesus claimed to be the Messiah, the Son of God. Since Jesus claimed equality with God, that leaves me with only three options. He was either a liar, a lunatic, or the Lord who He claimed to be." Well, she didn't like any of those options. She said she believed Him to be "a great teacher of faith in God, but not equal to God." But I replied, "He didn't leave that option open for us. He said He was equal with God. He either lied about that statement, and was deceitful, or He actually believed He was God but was crazy, or else He really *was* God. There are no other options." I'm not sure we got a convert that day, but she was doing some serious thinking.

I like what C.S. Lewis writes about this subject: "I am trying here to prevent anyone saying the really foolish thing that people often say about Him: 'I'm ready to accept Jesus as a great moral teacher, but I don't accept His claim to be God.' That is the one thing we must not say. A man who was merely a man and said the sort of things Jesus said would not be a great moral teacher. He would either be a lunatic—on a level with the man who says he is a poached egg—or else he would be the Devil of Hell. You must make your choice. Either this man was, and is, the Son of God, or else a madman or something worse."

Then Lewis adds, "You can shut Him up for a fool, you can spit at Him and kill Him as a demon; or you can fall at His feet and call Him Lord and God. But let us not come up with any patronising nonsense about His being a great human teacher. He has not left that open to us. He did not intend to."*

CHALLENGE

How does the quote by C.S. Lewis make you feel about your faith in Jesus Christ? Are you living as if Jesus is the Lord of your life?

---

* C.S. Lewis, *Mere Christianity* (New York: MacMillan, 1960), p. 56.

DAY 7

The Influence of One Life

*God exalted him to the highest place and gave
him the name that is above every name, that at
the name of Jesus every knee should bow, in
heaven and on earth and under the earth, and
every tongue confess that Jesus Christ is Lord, to
the glory of God the Father.*

—Philippians 2:9-11

Today millions and millions of people worship
Jesus Christ. Their language may be different from
yours, and even their approach to worship will
vary in every culture and denomination. But when
all is said and done, the influence of our Lord Jesus
Christ has affected life on this earth more than that
of all other men or religions combined. Today in
every part of the world people kneel before Him;
like you and I, they stand amazed at His influence
in our world. These beautiful words help us understand the powerful influence of this one life.

Here is a man who was born in an obscure village, the child of a peasant woman. He grew up in another village. He worked in a carpenter shop until He was thirty, and then for three years He was an itinerant preacher. He never wrote a book. He never held office. He never owned a home. He never had a family. He never went to college. He never put His feet inside a big city. He never traveled 200 miles from the place where He was born. He never did one of the things that usually accompany greatness. He had no credentials but Himself.

While still a young man, the tide of popular opinion turned against Him. His friends ran away. One of them denied Him. He was turned over to His enemies. He went through the mockery of a trial. He was nailed upon a cross between two thieves. His executioners gambled for the only piece of property He had on earth while He was dying, and that was His coat. When He was dead He was taken down and laid in a borrowed grave through the pity of a friend.

Nineteen wide centuries have come and gone, and today He is the centerpiece of the human race and the leader of the column of progress.

I am far within the mark when I say that all the armies that ever marched, and all

the navies that were ever built, and all
the parliaments that ever sat, and all the
kings that ever reigned, put together have
not affected the life of man upon this
earth as has that one solitary life.*

CHALLENGE

The influence of Jesus Christ transcends our ability to understand it all. Take a few moments to pause and reflect on His greatness and majesty. He is your King, He is your Savior, He is your Lord.

* Author unknown.

GOD'S FAITHFUL PROMISES

DAY 1

He Makes Your Weakness His Strength

He said to me, "My grace is sufficient for you, for my power is made perfect in weakness." Therefore I will boast all the more gladly about my weaknesses, so that Christ's power may rest on me.

—2 Corinthians 12:9

I asked God for strength that I might achieve.
I was made weak that I might learn humbly to obey.

I asked God for health that I might do great things.
I was given infirmity that I might do better things.

I asked for riches that I might be happy.
I was given poverty that I might be wise.

I asked for power that I might have the praise of men.

I was given weakness that I might feel
   the need of God.

I asked for all things that I might enjoy
   life.
I was given life that I might enjoy all
   things.

I got nothing I asked for
   but everything I had hoped for...

Almost despite myself my unspoken
   prayers were answered.

I am among all men most richly
   blessed.*

An unknown confederate soldier wrote these powerful words. He knew the truth of today's Scripture: It's not *what you have* but *who you know*. Paul wrote another thought about weakness that you should know about: "'The foolishness of God is wiser than man's wisdom, and the weakness of God is stronger than man's strength" (1 Corinthians 1:25). Don't be afraid in your weakest moments to lean on the strong and steady arms of your Savior!

CHALLENGE

Today give a weakness to God and ask Him to turn it into a strength. It won't be easy, and you'll have to give God the credit.

---

* Tim Hansel, *When I Relax I Feel Guilty* (Elgin: David C. Cook, 1979), p. 89.

DAY 2

Hope in the Midst of Hassles

I am convinced that neither death nor life, neither angels nor demons, neither the present nor the future, nor any powers, neither height nor depth, nor anything else in all creation, will be able to separate us from the love of God that is in Christ Jesus our Lord.

—Romans 8:38,39

If you read today's headlines in the newspaper you can get pretty depressed. Yes, at times life looks pretty hopeless. But if we keep our eyes on our Lord Jesus Christ we can have hope even in the midst of difficult circumstances. We can be comforted by Paul's words found in Romans 8:31: "If God is for us, who can be against us?" God is for you, and through His love you can find hope!

Here are four reasons why you can remain hopeful in the midst of confusing circumstances.

1. *Jesus will win the final victory.*
One day an old janitor was sitting in the
gymnasium of a theological seminary
reading the book of Revelation. One of
the young theologians sat down beside
him and asked him, "Do you understand
all the symbolism?" The janitor replied,
"No, absolutely not, but I have figured
out that *Jesus wins*, and that's comforting
to know 'cause I'm on His side."

Jesus told these words to the apostle John:
"I am the Alpha and the Omega, the
Beginning and the End. To him who is
thirsty I will give to drink without cost
from the spring of the water of life"
(Revelation 21:6).

2. *Jesus sets you free.*
Jesus said, "You will know the truth and
the truth will set you free." In Christ you
can have hope because you have been set
free from your sin. You are free to be all
that God desires you to be without the
constraints of your past. You can know
the meaning of abundant life because of
what Christ did for you on the cross.

3. *There is no condemnation for those in
Christ.*
In Christ you are a new creation. Romans
8:1,2 puts it best: "There is now no condemnation for those who are in Christ
Jesus, because through Christ Jesus the
law of the Spirit of life set me free from

the law of sin and death." Even though we deserve death and spiritual separation from God, we have new beginnings and eternal life in Jesus Christ. Talk about a reason for hope!

4. *God's love transcends human understanding.*
Because God loves us, we are "more than conquerors" (Romans 8:37) through Christ. God loves you and wants the best for you. His love will give you hope even in the bleakest of circumstances. There is a light always shining, and the light is the love of God. In Him you can find hope.

CHALLENGE

Make a list of reasons why you can be hopeful in a world filled with hopeless happenings. Remember: Keeping your eyes on Christ will keep your hope alive!

DAY 3

Satisfaction Guaranteed

Blessed are those who hunger and thirst for righteousness, for they shall be satisfied.
—Matthew 5:6 RSV

There is a great promise in today's verse. If you hunger and thirst for righteousness you will be *satisfied*. In order to be satisfied you've got to pursue righteousness with everything you have. God wants our 100-percent effort. Why is it that I'll give my 100-percent effort on the tennis court or when planning a party, but when it comes to pursuing righteousness, sometimes I coast? When I'm not giving God my best, an empty feeling creeps into my life. Today's promise in Matthew 5:6 challenges me to pull out the stops, roll up my sleeves, and with reckless abandon dive into the arms of the Savior. If I pursue with all my heart and energy what God has placed on my heart, the result will be *satisfaction.*

I like what Charles Paul Conn wrote:

Whatever it is,
However impossible it seems,
Whatever the obstacle that lies between
   you and it,
If it is noble,
If it is consistent with God's kingdom,
You must hunger after it
And stretch yourself to reach it.*

CHALLENGE

What would you do with your life if you knew you couldn't fail? Do you pursue God like a hungry army after a great battle or like a child picking at his plate, not satisfied but casually interested in the food? Grab ahold of today's promise and *go for it!*

---

* Ted W. Engstrom, *The Pursuit of Excellence* (Grand Rapids: Zondervan, 1982), p. 21.

He Is Always with You

It is the Lord who goes before you; he will be with you, he will not fail you or forsake you; do not fear or be dismayed.

—Deuteronomy 31:8 RSV

One night a man had a dream. He dreamed he was walking along the beach with the Lord. Across the sky flashed scenes from his life. For each scene he noticed two sets of footprints in the sand: one belonging to him, and the other to the Lord.

When the last scene of his life flashed before him, he looked back at the footprints in the sand. He noticed that many times along the path of his life there was only one set of footprints. He also noticed that it happened at the very lowest and saddest times in his life.

This really bothered him, and he
questioned the Lord about it. "Lord,
You said that once I decided to follow
You, You'd walk with me all the way.
But I have noticed that during the most
troublesome times in my life, there is
only one set of footprints. I don't
understand why when I needed You
most You would leave me."

The Lord replied, "My precious,
precious child, I love you and I would
never leave you. During your times of
trial and suffering, when you see only
one set of footprints, it was then that I
carried you."

—Author Unknown

When you feel discouraged, take heart: God's
promise to never leave you or forsake you is
always there to get you through your troubles.
Why is it that we tend to turn to Him as the last
resort when He is always faithfully by our side?

Psalm 23 can be such an encouragement in times
of trouble! Take a fresh look at this famous psalm
and be comforted that God has walked with you
through your dark days.

The Lord is my shepherd; I shall not
    want.
He makes me lie down in green pastures;
    he leads me beside the still waters.
He restores my soul.
He leads me in the paths of righteousness
    for his name's sake.

Even though I walk through the valley of
   the shadow of death,
   I will fear no evil,
   for thou art with me:
   thy rod and thy staff,
   they comfort me.

Thou preparest a table before me
   in the presence of my enemies;
   thou anointest my head with oil;
   my cup runneth over.

Surely goodness and mercy shall follow
   me
   all the days of my life,
   and I will dwell in the house of the
   Lord forever.*

CHALLENGE

How can you be reassured of God's constant faithfulness to you? Reread Psalm 23 and commit it to memory!

---

* KJV (emended).

DAY 5

A Reservoir of Power

You will receive power when the Holy Spirit comes on you; and you will be my witnesses in Jerusalem, and in all Judea and Samaria, and to the ends of the earth.

—Acts 1:8

I heard a story a few years ago about a farmer in the panhandle of Texas. This farmer and his wife had eked out a meager living in the dusty panhandle for 30 years when an impeccably dressed man in a three-piece suit driving a fancy car came to their door. He told the farmer that he had good reason to believe there was a reservoir of oil underneath his property. If the farmer would allow the gentleman the right to drill, perhaps the farmer would become a wealthy man. The farmer stated emphatically that he didn't want anyone messing up his property and asked the gentleman to leave.

The next year about the same time the gentleman returned again with his nice clothes and another fancy car. The oilman pleaded with the farmer, and again the farmer said no. This same experience went on for the next eight years. During those eight years the farmer and his wife really struggled to make ends meet. Nine years after the first visit from the oilman, the farmer came down with a disease that put him in the hospital. When the gentleman arrived to plead his case for oil he spoke to the farmer's wife. Reluctantly she gave permission to drill.

Within a week huge oil rigs were beginning the process of drilling for oil. The first day nothing happened. The second day was filled with only disappointment and dust. But on the third day, right about noon, black bubbly liquid began to squirt up in the air. The oilman had found "black gold," and the farmer and his wife were instantly millionaires.

You have a reservoir of power in your life. If you are a Christian, the Holy Spirit works in your life. You can tap into His power and live your life with resurrection power. The Holy Spirit will empower you to live life on a greater level, but you've got to tap into His power source just like the farmer needed to drill for oil. The Bible says to "be filled with the Spirit" (Ephesians 5:18) and to "live by the Spirit" (Galatians 5:16). People are searching for the power to change their lives when in fact the power is already dwelling within them in the form of God's Holy Spirit. Tap into His reservoir of power!

CHALLENGE

Take a moment today to allow the Holy Spirit to take control of your life and actions. When God's Spirit is ruling your life, you're in for a great adventure!

DAY 6

Taste and See
for Yourself

*Delight yourself in the Lord and he will give
you the desires of your heart.*

—Psalm 37:4

When you've tasted all that the Lord has to offer,
it is difficult to settle for rubbish. If God is our
Creator and Christ is who the Bible claims Him to
be, then you can come into His fullness and not be
disappointed. When confronted with the truth,
even skeptics who doubt the Christian faith
respond to the goodness and knowledge of God.

Lew Wallace was a famous literary critic and a
general during the Civil War. He believed that
Christianity kept people in ignorance, fear, superstitions, and bondage. One Sunday morning while
riding a train he observed hundreds of people going
to Sunday worship. He decided to research and
write a book that would forever liberate Christian
people from their ignorance and superstitions. For

two years Wallace studied in leading libraries of Europe and America to disclaim Christianity forever. He finished the study and began to write. He wrote his first chapter, and as he was laboring over his second chapter he suddenly found himself on his knees saying, "My Lord and my God!" The One whom he had set out to disprove had captured him. Lew Wallace became a devout follower of Christ and authored the great Christian classic *Ben Hur*. "Taste and see that the Lord is good!"

CHALLENGE

Don't be afraid to ask questions or seek knowledge about your faith in God. As you search and experience God, you will only become more convinced of His faithfulness and reality in your life.

DAY 7

used in Pulse
8-99

Hang on to Hope

Since we are surrounded by such a great cloud of witnesses, let us throw off everything that hinders and the sin that so easily entangles, and let us run with perseverance the race marked out for us. Let us fix our eyes on Jesus, the author and perfecter of our faith, who for the joy set before him endured the cross, scorning its shame, and sat down at the right hand of the throne of God.

—Hebrews 12:1,2

Do you ever feel like a failure? Some people look at the life of Jesus and say that He failed. He was born in obscurity. For most of His life He was a lonely carpenter. For three years He traveled as an itinerant preacher, and for those three years of effort He really didn't have many disciples and no substantial following to speak of. He died in shame with two common prisoners alongside Him. If the story stopped here, all would consider Him a failure. But the story continues, because three days later He *rose from the dead*, ascending into heaven and now sitting at the right hand of our Father!

If you feel like a failure, you're in good company. Abraham Lincoln had more failures than victories, yet some would call him the greatest president the United States has ever had. Look at his life for a moment. He grew up on an isolated farm with only one year of formal education. In his early years he was exposed to barely half-a-dozen books. In 1832 he lost his job and was defeated in the race for the Illinois legislature. In 1833 he failed in business. In 1834 he was elected to the state legislature, but in 1835 his sweetheart died, and in 1836 he had a nervous breakdown. In 1838 he was defeated for Speaker of the House, and in 1843 he was defeated for nomination for Congress. In 1846 he was elected to Congress but in 1848 lost the renomination. In 1849 he was rejected for a federal land officer appointment, and in 1854 he was defeated for the Senate. In 1856 he was defeated for the nomination of Vice President, and in 1858 was again defeated for the Senate.*

Was Lincoln a failure? Absolutely not! He became one of the greatest Presidents in the history of the United States.

There is one word that comes to mind when I think of failure: *perseverance*. To persevere means to hang on, to stick with it, to press forward! The call of the Christian is to keep on looking to Jesus and moving in His direction. You can rest assured that the Bible is right when it says, "He who began a good work in you will carry it on to completion

---

* Ted W. Engstrom, *The Pursuit of Excellence* (Grand Rapids: Zondervan, 1982), p. 57.

until the day of Christ Jesus" (Philippians 1:6). So hang on—there is light at the end of the tunnel, and the light is the love of Christ!

CHALLENGE

Do you see God's hand in any of your failures? In what area of your life do you need to persevere? Be reminded today of God's promise that He will complete the good work He began in you. You're on the right road if you're putting your trust in Jesus!

SERVANTHOOD

DAY 1

You Are the Only Jesus Somebody Knows

I have been crucified with Christ and I no longer live, but Christ lives in me. The life I live in the body, I live by faith in the Son of God, who loved me and gave himself for me.
—Galatians 2:20

There was a soldier who was wounded in battle. The padre crept out and did what he could for him. He stayed with him when the remainder of the troops retreated. In the heat of the day he gave him water from his own waterbottle, while he himself remained parched with thirst. In the night, when the chill frost came down, he covered the wounded man with his own coat, and finally wrapped him up in even more of his own clothes to save him from the cold. In the end the wounded man looked up at the padre. "Padre," he said, "you're a Christian?" "I try to be," said the padre.

"Then," said the wounded man, "if Christianity makes a man do for another man what you have done for me, tell me about it, because I want it."*

You are the only Jesus somebody knows. Christ lives in you and will use you to help heal this hurting world if you'll let Him. The priest was willing to become uncomfortable for the sake of a dying man. Sometimes I don't feel like going out of my way to reach out to someone and sometimes I close the door. There are other times when I realize that I represent Jesus to the world around me and that I touch someone not with *my* love but with *His* love. And it makes a difference in their life...and mine.

CHALLENGE

Ask God to give you a person to reach out to today. The odds are great that sometime during your day you'll see who He wanted to touch through you. Go ahead and ask Him!

---

* William Barclay, *The Letter to the Romans* (Philadelphia: Westminster Press, 1975), p. 148.

DAY 2

Responding with Love

Do nothing out of selfish ambition or vain conceit, but in humility consider others better than yourselves. Each of you should look not only to your own interests, but also to the interests of others.

—Philippians 2:3,4

Babe Ruth is one of my heroes. He hit 714 home runs during his baseball career. But along with being the home-run king he was also the strikeout king. In one of Babe's last major league games the Braves played the Cincinnati Reds. The great Babe Ruth was no longer as agile as he had once been. His game that day was filled with costly errors and strikeouts.

As the Babe walked off the field after a dismal inning, the crowd stood and booed their disapproval of his play. Just then a little boy jumped over the railing onto the playing field. With tears streaming down his face he threw his arms around the legs of his hero. Ruth didn't hesitate for a moment. He picked up the boy and gave him a hug. Suddenly the booing stopped and a hush fell over the entire ballpark. In that brief moment the baseball fans saw two heroes: Ruth, who in spite of his horrible day still cared about a little boy, and the small child, who cared about the feelings of another human being. Both had melted the hearts of the crowd.

How is your sensitivity toward other people? Do you take time to care about the needs of your friends and family? Sometimes we get so absorbed with our own personal problems we forget that there is a hurting world around us that needs our attention. The strange thing about it is that when we give love and concern to others, we usually forget about our own problems! Make someone feel special today.

CHALLENGE

Who can you make feel like royalty today? What little act of kindness can you do to make his or her day a little brighter? Don't hesitate to respond with love.

DAY 3

The Road to Happiness

*They came to Capernaum. When he was in the
house, he asked them, "What were you arguing
about on the road?" But they kept quiet because
on the way they had argued about who was the
greatest.*

*Sitting down, Jesus called the Twelve and said,
"If anyone wants to be first, he must be the very
last, and the servant of all."*

—Mark 9:33-35

We live in a self-absorbed, self-centered world.
That's why there is so much unhappiness in the
world. It seems to me that happy people are
others-centered people and that unhappy people
tend to be I-centered. The Bible constantly
challenges us to be a servant, to think of others
rather than ourselves. Albert Schweitzer was a
person who knew a lot about serving. He was a

missionary doctor in Africa for years. Here's what he had to say about becoming a servant.

> I don't know
> what your destiny will be,
> but one thing I know—
> the only ones among you
> who will be really happy
> are those who have sought
> and found how to serve.

If you've been feeling unhappy and unfulfilled lately, perhaps it's time to take an evaluation of your life. Are you I-centered or others-centered? Your decision will affect your destiny. The road to happiness is the road of service.

CHALLENGE

What can you do to become a greater servant? Ask God to put a person or a cause in your life which you can serve. As you serve you'll find happiness in your own life as well as put happiness in the lives of others.

DAY 4

You Serve Jesus by Serving His Children

The King will reply, "I tell you the truth, whatever you did for one of the least of these brothers of mine, you did for me."

—Matthew 25:40

Martin of Tours was a Roman soldier and a Christian.

One cold winter day, as he was entering a city, a beggar stopped him and asked for alms; Martin had no money, but the beggar was blue and shivering with cold, and Martin gave what he had. He took off his soldier's coat, worn and frayed as it was; he cut it in two and gave half of it to the beggar man. That night he had a dream. In it he saw the heavenly places and all the angels and Jesus in the midst of them; and Jesus was wearing half a

73

Roman soldier's cloak. One of the angels said to him, "Master, why are you wearing that battered old cloak? Who gave it to you?" And Jesus answered softly, "My servant Martin gave it to me."*

This Scripture and story bring a chill to my body when I read it. I feel two opposite emotions. I want to run and care for every person I see as if they were Jesus, and I want to run and hide in selfishness and self-pity and not touch a soul with my life. The choice is mine to make. I think I'll try to see the Jesus in each person, and I think I'll ask God to help me see, with the eyes of Jesus, each person's needs. How about you?

CHALLENGE

Who in your life needs you to give him or her an extra dose of love today? What practical experience can you do today to serve Jesus by serving one of His children?

---

* William Barclay, *The Gospel of Matthew* (Philadelphia: Westminster Press, 1975), p. 326.

You Are a Representative of Christ on Earth

You are the body of Christ, and each one of you is a part of it.

—1 Corinthians 12:27

God created the world
He appeared on this earth in the form
  of Jesus Christ
He was beautiful
We mocked Him and killed Him.

He rose from the dead
He is alive and eternal
He needs a new body on this earth.
You've been chosen!

You are an important part of the body of Christ. You are needed to fulfill His work on earth. Your job is to live as He lived and to love as He loved. One other thing: He gives you His Spirit to get you through your day.

CHALLENGE

Did you know that you are the only Jesus somebody knows? Today love someone as Jesus would love him.

DAY 6

You Are the Hands of Christ

You are the body of Christ, and each one of you is a part of it.
                                    —1 Corinthians 12:27

If you are a Christian, then you are a part of the body of Christ on earth. It's your hands and legs and mouth that He uses to do His daily tasks in your world.

In Alexander Irvine's novel *My Lady of the Chimney Corner,* an old woman went to comfort a neighbor whose boy lay dead. She laid her hand on her friend's head and said, "Ah, wuman, God isn't a printed book to be carried aroun' by a man in fine clothes, not a cross danglin' at the watch chain of a priest. God takes a hand wherever he can find it.... Sometimes he takes a Bishop's hand and lays it on a child's head in benediction, the hand of a doctor to relieve pain, the hand of a mother to guide a child, and sometimes he takes the hand of a poor old wuman like me to give comfort to a neighbor. But they're all hands touched by His Spirit, and His Spirit is everywhere lukin' for his hands to use."*

God's Spirit is looking for hands, bodies, and minds to use. But He seldom uses us without our permission. We, like Isaiah, have to first say, "Here I am, Lord—send me." That is precisely what God wants you to say in order to start your great adventure of service. Some people you know will spend their lives totally self-absorbed and will miss the greatest opportunity of life, which is to make a difference in our world.

CHALLENGE

Can you say like Isaiah, "Here I am, Lord—send me"? When a Christian asks God to use him or her, God usually complies with that request. Is there anything more exciting or important in life than to be used by God to do His work on earth?

---

* Alexander Irvine, *My Lady of the Chimney Corner* (Flint: Apple Tree Press, 1981).

DAY 7

Make Me an Instrument

He said to his disciples, "The harvest is
plentiful but the workers are few."
—Matthew 9:37

Francis of Assisi was a wealthy, highborn man who lived hundreds of years ago. He felt that his life was incomplete, and even though he had more than enough wealth he was a very unhappy man. One day while he was out riding he met a leper. The leper was loathsome and repulsive in the ugliness of his disease. Something moved Francis to dismount and fling his arms around this person. In the arms of Francis the leper's face changed to the face of Christ. Francis was never the same again.

Francis of Assisi spent the rest of his life serving his Lord Jesus Christ. He wrote these famous words as a prayer to God from the heart of a man who had a deep desire to be an instrument of God's will on this earth.

Lord, make me an instrument of Your
    peace.
Where there is hatred,
    let me sow love;
    where there is injury, pardon;
    where there is doubt, faith;
    where there is despair, hope;
    where there is darkness, light;
    and where there is sadness, joy.

CHALLENGE

Can you say these words to God as your sincere
prayer? There is nothing greater than to be an
instrument of God's will for His kingdom.

DAY 1

Costly Discipleship

He called the crowd to him along with his disciples and said: "If anyone would come after me, he must deny himself and take up his cross and follow me. For whoever wants to save his life will lose it, but whoever loses his life for me and for the gospel will save it. What good is it for a man to gain the whole world, yet forfeit his soul?"
—Mark 8:34-36

To pick up the cross and follow Jesus means to be willing to go anywhere and do anything for your Lord. It means that you want God to do His will in and through you. There is a cost to being a disciple of Jesus Christ, but the end results are well worth it. I recently heard of a business executive who said, "I spent my entire life climbing the corporate ladder only to find when I got to the top that my ladder was leaning against the wrong building. I have wasted my life with trivia."

Are you passionately pursuing Christ? Don't waste your life in a trivial pursuit when you have at your fingertips the Lord of life to guide you into greater depths and a more meaningful lifestyle.

To be a disciple of Jesus means to pursue Him like the pursuit of a lover and the passion of a romance. Christ is worth your every thought and breath. In Him you will find your reason for living. Remember that He gives you His Spirit but wants you to give Him your body, mind, and soul.

CHALLENGE

What does it mean for you to deny yourself, take up your cross, and follow Jesus? What will it take to be His disciple? Are you willing to pay the price of discipleship? The decision is yours.

Choose to Be Different

I came that they may have life, and have it abundantly.

—John 10:10 RSV

Once upon a time in a land far away there lived a group of people called the Laconians. The Laconians lived in a rural setting; their village was surrounded by a forest. They looked and acted a lot like you and I do. They dressed like we dress and went to school and work like we do. They even had the same family struggles and search for identity that we have. But there was one major difference: Connected to the ankle of every Laconian was a brace, and attached to the brace was a strong metal chain, and connected to the chain was a round, heavy metal ball.

Wherever the Laconians went or whatever they did, they carried the ball and chain. Yet no one seemed to mind. After all, they were used to the ball and chain, and no one in Laconia was free from the bondage of the ball and chain.

One day the hero of the story, Tommy, was in the forest after school exploring when he went around a corner, slipped, and fell—and the chain broke. Tommy had never heard of a chain breaking before in the land of Laconia, and he was terrified. But he was also curious. As he stood and stared at the broken chain he sensed that something very significant had happened in his life. In fact he tried to take a step without the ball and chain and almost fell down. After all, he wasn't used to the freedom of walking without this bondage.

Tommy quickly slipped the ball and chain back on his ankle. He told no one of his new discovery. The next day after school this new curiosity drove him back to the forest to experiment with his new-found freedom. This time when he unhooked the chain he walked. Yes, it was wobbly, but he quickly learned to compensate, and in a few hours he was running and jumping and even trying to climb the trees in the forest. Every day after school he found himself out in the forest, free to experience life in a different way from anyone else in Laconia.

He decided to share his secret with his best friend. After school one day he brought his friend to the forest and showed him his new freedom. But his friend responded by saying, "Don't be different! Once a Laconian, you'll always be a Laconian. Be happy with what you have." This response only put more fuel in Tommy's fire. He knew he needed to show all the people of his little village that they could be set free.

One spring day when the whole village was outside, Tommy took the ball and placed it under his arm, then ran and skipped through the town. He wanted to show the people of his village his joy and freedom. Their response was that of shock. They mocked him, scolded him, and challenged him to not be different. Even his family told him to immediately become a normal part of the community, and put back his chain.

Tommy knew then and there that since he had experienced this freedom he could never again settle for second-best in life. For Tommy, mediocrity was out of the question. He would choose to be different... and he *was* different from then on.

I wrote this little story for people who don't want to settle for second-best in life. What is keeping you from breaking the chain and striving to be all that God wants you to be? Jesus said, "You will know the truth, and the truth will set you free." You don't have to live a life of boring mediocrity. God's desire for your life is to break the chain that holds you back and to give your life to His purpose. You can choose to be different!

CHALLENGE

Do you need to make a decision to break the chain that keeps you from giving your life to God's purpose? Identify which parts of your life are holding you back, and then yield those parts of your life to God's purpose!

DAY 3

Who's in Control?

What good is it for man to gain the whole world, yet forfeit his soul?

—Mark 8:36

When it comes to our life, we have no say about our birth and little say about our death, but in between these two events most of the decisions are ours to be made. Are you letting life and circumstances control you, or are you with God's help controlling your own life and destiny? Don't let life pass you by when you have the God-given ability to make things happen. I've heard it said:

You can't control the length of your life,
    but you can control its use.

You can't control your facial appearance,
    but you can control its expression.

You can't control the weather, but you
    can control the moral atmosphere that
    surrounds you.

You can't control the distance of your head above the ground, but you can control the height of the contents in your head.

You can't control the other fellow's annoying faults, but you can see to it that you do not develop similar faults.

Why worry about things you cannot control? Get busy controlling the things that depend on *you*.

CHALLENGE

What decision must you make to allow God to control your life? Have you been letting life pass you by, or have you been making things happen? Who's in control?

DAY 4

The Pressure to Compromise

*What then? Shall we sin because we are not
under law but under grace? By no means! Don't
you know that when you offer yourselves to someone to obey him as slaves, you are slaves to the
one whom you obey—whether you are slaves to
sin, which leads to death, or to obedience, which
leads to righteousness?*

—Romans 6:15,16

The pressure to compromise our lifestyle is one
of the greatest battles that comes our way. We all
experience peer pressure, no matter what our age.
The pressure to compromise makes a five-year-old
scream a dirty word or a 16-year-old get drunk at a
party. The same pressure forces a business executive to cheat on a business deal and then say,
"Everyone does it."

A Christian is called to stand firm and not be
seduced by peer pressure, even though sometimes

it is very difficult to stand out in the crowd. Most of the time you'll feel better for keeping your principles, though there might be times when you will lose a friend, a job, or some other situation. Christians are always called to stand on the side of righteousness even if it is unpopular to do so.

If you have trouble in withstanding the pressure to compromise, here are three principles that will help you through your day:

1. Everyone you spend time with has an influence on you. Choose your friends wisely.

2. Remember your uniqueness. You are special in God's eyes.

3. Seek first the kingdom of God. Pleasing God is better than pleasing your friends.

Make Micah 6:8 a verse to live by:

He has showed you, O man, what is good. And what does the Lord require of you? To act justly and to love mercy and to walk humbly with your God.

CHALLENGE

What areas in your life are vulnerable to compromise? This week stand firm. Stand for righteousness. Ask the question, "What would Jesus want me to do?"

DAY 5

The Secret of Endurance

*In this you greatly rejoice, though now for a
little while you may have had to suffer grief in all
kinds of trials. These have come so that your
faith—of greater worth than gold, which perishes
even though refined by fire—may be proved
genuine and may result in praise, glory and honor
when Jesus Christ is revealed.*

—1 Peter 1:6,7

There is no doubt that you will experience trials
in your Christian life. Some new Christians mis-
takenly believe that being a Christian means living
a life free of hassles and struggles. God never
promised us freedom from trials; He promised us
that He would walk with us through the trials and
help us to endure our hardships.

No one looks forward to trials, but trials can pro-
duce a stronger faith. You can withstand anything
that comes if you remember that every trial is

actually a test. Before gold is pure it must be tested in the fire. The trials which come your way will test your faith, and out of your struggles your faith can emerge stronger than it ever was before.

The rigors which the athlete has to undergo are not meant to make him collapse but to help him develop strength and staying power. For the Christian, our trials are not meant to take the strength *out of* us, but to put the strength *into* us. Endurance through trials produces strength.

CHALLENGE

Are you going through a struggle in your life that really has you down? How about looking at this trial as a testing of your faith? What can you do to make this struggling experience a positive step of faith?

DAY 6

You Are a Daily Gospel to the World

*I have been crucified with Christ, and I no
longer live, but Christ lives in me. The life I live
in the body, I live by faith in the Son of God,
who loved me and gave himself for me.*
                              —Galatians 2:20

Your life is not your own; you were bought with
a price—the high price and sacrifice of Jesus on
the cross at Calvary. Although you may look the
same and even have the same personality and man-
nerisms, on the inside you become a new person
when Jesus Christ enters your life. You become a
representative of your Lord wherever you go.

A little poem has always helped me understand
that my new life in Christ is a daily gospel
to the world. I am saying, as Paul said, "I
have been crucified with Christ, and I no longer
live, but Christ lives in me. The life I live in
the body, I live by faith in the Son of God, who

loves me and gave himself for me."
Here's the poem:

> You are writing a gospel,
> A chapter each day,
> By deeds that you do,
> By words that you say.
> Men read what you write,
> Whether faithless or true,
> Say, what is the gospel according to you?*

CHALLENGE

What has your personal gospel looked like today or even yesterday? "Gospel" means "good news." Is your life *good news and hope* to someone who needs it? Today try to make your life a gospel!

---

* Author unknown, *The Spice of Life* (Norwalk: C.R. Gibson Co.), p. 29.

Your Best Interest Is His Best Interest

He called the crowd to him along with his disciples and said: "If anyone would come after me, he must deny himself and take up his cross and follow me."

—Mark 8:34

I recently read of a man who bought a hotel in Spokane, Washington. There was only one problem: The hotel's restaurant was the big money-maker, since the bar grossed 10,000 dollars a month. But the new owner wasn't going to keep the bar. It's not that he wanted to impose his own views on other people, but as a Christian he chose not to run a business subsidized by alcohol sales. The hotel manager argued with the new owner that if guests couldn't drink they would be out the door to a competitor. He also gave the new owner some convincing statistics showing that he couldn't make it financially without the bar. The owner listened politely and closed the door to the bar. He had to stick to his convictions. The manager promptly quit.

The owner remodeled the hotel lobby and turned the bar into a cozy coffee shop. In the first couple of years of business, food sales went up 20 percent and room bookings were up 30 percent. Still, profits weren't what they could be if the bar were open.

But the hotel owner's reply was, "Beliefs aren't worth much if a fella's not ready to live by them!"

CHALLENGE

Are you willing to deny yourself in order to follow the call of Jesus? Don't let anyone kid you—there is a sense of self-denial when you get serious with getting in touch with God.

DAY 1

You Are Special

You created my inmost being; you knit me together in my mother's womb. I praise you because I am fearfully and wonderfully made; your works are wonderful, I know that full well. My frame was not hidden from you when I was made in the secret place. When I was woven together in the depths of the earth, your eyes saw my unformed body. All the days ordained for me were written in your book before one of them came to be.

—Psalm 139:13-16

You are unique. You are special. God created you, and there is not another person in the world exactly like you. True, there are things about us that we really don't like. I wish I were taller, richer, and more intelligent. There are some aspects of our lives that we can work on to improve and other aspects that we must learn to accept. The people who learn to accept the good with the bad are the ones who find happiness. Cathy and I have

97

a prayer hung up in our bathroom that helps me when I'm feeling less than good about myself and the circumstances in my life. It simply reads:

> God grant me the serenity
> to accept the things I cannot change,
> courage to change those I can,
> and wisdom to know the difference.

Great advice for those who sometimes forget they are special in the eyes of God!

CHALLENGE

Is there something in your life you've been struggling to accept and need to realize that you'll live with for the rest of your life? Or is there something in your life you could change if you had the courage and fortitude?

You Can Fly!

I tell you the truth, anyone who has faith in me will do what I have been doing. He will do even greater things than these, because I am going to the Father. And I will do whatever you ask in my name, so that the Son may bring glory to the Father. You may ask me for anything in my name, and I will do it.

—John 14:12-14

Soren Kierkegaard tells a story about a make-believe country where only ducks live.

On Sunday morning all the ducks came into church, waddled down the aisle, waddled into their pews, and squatted. Then the duck minister came in, took his place behind the pulpit, opened his duck Bible and read, "Ducks! You have wings, and with wings, you can fly like eagles. You can soar into the sky! Ducks! You have wings!" All the ducks yelled,

"Amen!" and then they waddled home.*

The ducks could fly, but they settled for waddling instead. Many Christians are like those ducks: They attend church regularly and even know what the Bible has to say about living the abundant life of a committed Christian, but they never get around to acting upon their belief.

You can fly! You can soar above the clouds of mediocrity and become all that God has in store for you! Paul said, "I can do all things through Him who strengthens me." Jesus said, "Whatever you ask in prayer, believe that you have received it, and it will be yours." James said, "You do not have because you do not ask."

Has God put a dream or idea in your mind? With Christ you can accomplish that desire. You can make a difference in your world. You can fly!

CHALLENGE

Today's Scripture promises that you will do great works for God. He gives you the insight and power. You must have a willingness to move beyond the natural and into the supernatural realm of living.

---

* Tony Campolo, *You Can Make A Difference* (Waco: Word, 1984), p. 74.

DAY 3

Never Settle for Mediocrity

I am the vine; you are the branches. If a man remains in me and I in him, he will bear much fruit; apart from me you can do nothing.
                                    —John 15:5

Too many people today settle for second-best in life. Mediocrity is all they put into life, and mediocrity is all they get out of life. Yet Paul said, "I can do all things through Christ who strengthens me" (Philippians 4:13 NKJV). He doesn't sound like a person who chooses to be average, and you don't have to be average either.

There's an American Indian story about a brave who found an eagle's egg and put it into the nest of a prairie chicken. The eaglet hatched with the brood of chicks and grew up with them.

All his life the changeling eagle, thinking he was a prairie chicken, did what the prairie chickens did. He scratched in the dirt for seeds and insects to eat. He clucked and cackled. And he flew in a brief thrashing of wings and flurry of feathers no more than a few feet off the ground. After all, that's how prairie chickens were supposed to fly!

Years passed, and the changeling eagle grew very old. One day he saw a magnificent bird far above him in the cloudless sky. Hanging with graceful majesty on the powerful wind currents, it soared with scarcely a beat of its strong golden wings.

"What a beautiful bird!" said the changeling eagle to his neighbor. "What is it?"

"That's an eagle—the chief of the birds," the neighbor clucked. "But don't give it a second thought. You could never be like him."

So the changeling eagle never gave it another thought. And it died thinking it was a prairie chicken.*

CHALLENGE

You don't have to settle for second-best in life. God wants to help you soar through the clouds rather than settle for mediocrity. Are you willing today to commit to all that God has in store for you? If you are, then tell Him so right now.

---

* Anecdote retold from *What a Day This Can Be*, by John Cateior, ed., Director of The Christophers (New York: The Christophers).

DAY 4

God Draws Out the Best in You

*Just as you received Christ Jesus as Lord,
continue to live in him.*

—Colossians 2:6

Jesus had the power to draw out the best in people. He met a clumsy, big-mouthed fisherman named Simon. Jesus looked beyond Simon's present abilities and looked at his potential. He looked Simon straight in the eye and said, "So you are Simon the son of John?" Simon nodded. Jesus said, "You shall be called Peter."

"Peter" means "rock." Jesus nicknamed Simon Peter "The Rock." At the time Simon Peter was anything but a rock of a person. Yet Jesus saw his potential, and this fisherman became the rock-solid leader of the Jerusalem church.

Throughout the Bible we meet different individuals who had an encounter with God and became different people. *Abram* became *Abraham,* "the father of a multitude of nations." *Jacob* met God and became *Israel*, which means "soldier of God."

It is important for you to know that God affirms you as He affirmed Bible characters. He loves you and will draw out the best in you. He sees you not only for who you are but for who you can be.

CHALLENGE

Give God your insecurities and fears, and watch Him draw out the very best in you. God's affirmation will be the powerful change agent in your life. Let Him do His good work in your life!

DAY 5

You Are God's Poetry

We are God's workmanship, created in Christ Jesus to do good works, which God prepared in advance for us to do.

—Ephesians 2:10

Today's Scripture verse says, "We are God's workmanship." The word "workmanship" can be translated "poetry." Have you ever thought of yourself as one of God's special works of poetry? You are His special creation. You are unique. There is no one else in the whole world quite like you. You are an unrepeatable miracle.

When I'm feeling low I need to be reminded that I'm special in God's eyes. When I'm playing the comparison game and comparing my talent or physical appearance with those better than I am, I need to be reminded that God created me unique. When I'm playing the "I wish" game, wishing that things were different, I need to be reminded that I am the only special poem of God made just like me.

Many people today are so hard on themselves that they miss the joy of being God's only creation made from their unique mold. People who view themselves as God's special creation are the ones who live happy and successful lives. You are His poetry, so live your life as a child of God!

CHALLENGE

Do you have trouble liking who you are? If you do, it's time for a large dose of self-esteem rooted in Jesus Christ. Your first step is admitting and believing that you are God's special poem, His special and only creation made from your mold.

DAY 6

You Are What You Think

As he thinks in his heart, so is he.
— Proverbs 23:7 NKJV

Have you ever heard of the term "self-fulfilling prophecy?" A self-fulfilling prophecy is simply the truth of today's Scripture. You become what you think yourself to be. If you *think* you will fail, you probably will. If you *think* you will succeed, then most likely you will succeed.

Your mind is powerful. That's why Paul gives some excellent advice to the Philippian church that is still important for today.

> Finally, brothers, whatever is true, whatever is noble, whatever is right, whatever is pure, whatever is lovely, whatever is admirable—if anything is excellent or praiseworthy—think about such things. Whatever you have learned or received or

heard from me, or seen in me—put it into
practice. And the God of peace will be
with you (Philippians 4:8,9).

I'm afraid too many people's lives are a negative,
self-fulfilling prophecy when in Christ we can
become so much more. This little poem has helped
me focus my thoughts on Christ and on the positive side of self-fulfilling prophecy.

If you think you are beaten, you are.
If you think you dare not, you don't.
If you like to win, but think you can't,
it's almost a cinch you won't.

If you think you will lose, you are lost.
For out in the world we find
success begins with a fellow's will;
it's all in the state of mind.

Full many a race is lost
ere even a step is run,
and many a coward fails
ere even his work is begun.

Think big and your deed will grow;
think small and you will fall behind.
Think that you can and you will—
It's all in the state of mind.

If you think you are outclassed, you are.
You have got to think high to rise.
You have got to be sure of yourself
before you win a prize.

Life's battles don't always go
to the stronger or faster man.
But sooner or later the man who wins
is the man who thinks he can.

—Author Unknown

CHALLENGE

How would you rate your thought life? Does it bring you down, or does it lift you up? Pause for a moment and focus your thoughts on the power of Christ. The same resurrection power of Christ is yours for the asking!

Guilty!

All have sinned and fall short of the glory of God.

—Romans 3:23

The wages of sin is death, but the gift of God is eternal life in Christ Jesus our Lord.

—Romans 6:23

On a sunny September day a stern-faced, plainly dressed man stood on a street corner in downtown Chicago. Pedestrians hurried by on their way to lunch, shopping, or business. This solemn-faced man would lift his right arm, point to the person nearest him, and intone loudly the single word "GUILTY!"

Then, without any change of expression, he would resume his stiff stance for a few minutes before repeating the same gesture again, raising his arm and pointing to another person, then pronouncing loudly that one word "GUILTY!"

The effect that this strange man had on the people was almost eerie. People would stare at him, hesitate, look aside, and then hurry away as if they had been caught. One man turned to another man and exclaimed, "But how did he know?" Guilty! We are all guilty. We have made some major mistakes in our life, and many minor ones; we are all guilty.

When it comes to our relationship with God, we have all sinned and fallen short of His glory. To sin means to "miss the mark," and we have all missed the mark of God's perfection.

The good news is that sin and guilt are erased in Jesus Christ. There is a Scriptural principal which helps us understand the beauty of God's forgiveness of our sin and guilt. It's found in 1 John 1:9: "If we confess our sins, he is faithful and just and will forgive us our sins and purify us from all unrighteousness."

You don't have to live in the guilt of your past sins. You are forgiven. You are cleansed. Your sins are no longer remembered. Hallelujah!

CHALLENGE

Do you still feel guilt in your life? Take a few moments to claim God's forever forgiveness. Then rest assured that you can depend on His Word. To confess your sins to God actually means to agree with Him that you have "missed the mark" and are in need of His forgiveness. It's yours for the asking.

7 *OBEDIENCE*

DAY 1

Sometimes It Isn't Easy

*Love one another with brotherly affection; outdo
one another in showing honor.*
— Romans 12:10 RSV

No one ever said that living the Christian life would
be easy. The following words help give us perspective.

IT IS NOT EASY

To apologize.
To begin over.
To take advice.
To be unselfish.
To admit error.
To face a sneer.
To be charitable.
To keep trying.
To be considerate.
To avoid mistakes.
To endure success.
To profit by mistakes.

To forgive and forget.
To think and then act.
To keep out of a rut.
To make the best of little.
To subdue an unruly temper.
To shoulder a deserved blame.
BUT IT ALWAYS PAYS.

—Anonymous

CHALLENGE

How can this thought help you in relationships with other people today? Make a decision to "outdo one another in sharing honor." You'll be glad you did!

DAY 2

Slow Me Down, Lord

Seek first his kingdom and his righteousness, and all these things will be given to you as well. Therefore do not worry about tomorrow, for tomorrow will worry about itself. Each day has enough trouble of its own.

—Matthew 6:33,34

We live in a fast-paced society where at times we can become seduced by a culture that gets our mind off the Lord. To keep in touch with Jesus we must slow down our fierce pace and give Jesus our time and attention. This prayer has helped me for years with my tendency to overcommit my life to unimportant things and leave God on the sideline.

Slow me down, Lord.

Ease the pounding of my heart by the quieting of my mind.

Steady my hurried pace with a vision of the eternal reach of time.

Give me, amid the confusion of the day,
the calmness of the everlasting hills.

Break the tensions of my nerves and
muscles with the soothing music of the
singing streams that live in my memory.

Teach me the art of taking minute
vacations—of slowing down to look at a
flower, to chat with a friend, to pat a
dog, to smile at a child, to read a few
lines from a good book.

Slow me down, Lord, and inspire me to
send my roots deep into the soil of life's
enduring values, that I may grow
toward my greater destiny.

Remind me each day that the race is
not always to the swift; that there is
more to life than increasing its speed.

Let me look upward to the towering oak
and know that it grew great and strong
because it grew slowly and well.

—Orin D. Crain

CHALLENGE

Are your priorities in proper perspective? Take a
few minutes to give God your priorities and seek
His kingdom first.

DAY 3

A Hunger for Holiness

As obedient children, do not conform to the evil
desires you had when you lived in ignorance. But
just as he who called you is holy, so be holy in all
you do; for it is written: "Be holy, because I am
holy."

—1 Peter 1:14-16

Every Christian is called to live a life of holiness.
I'm afraid I've been guilty of wanting spectacular
results in my Christian life but giving only a medi-
ocre effort. Nobel prizewinner Mother Theresa put
it best when she said, "Our progress in holiness
depends on God and ourselves—on God's grace and
on our will to be holy." Pray today for a hunger
for holiness. Holiness means setting apart or purity.
Holiness is the everyday business of every Christian. It evidences itself in the decisions we make
and the lifestyle we live, hour by hour, day by day.
   Andrew Murray said, "The starting point and the
goal of our Christian life is obedience." Through
obedience to God and His Word your life will

become more holy. The goal to live a life of holiness is a lifelong process of sanctification and spiritual maturity. Some people never strive to become mature believers. The first step of holiness is a willingness to be obedient. The result of holiness is a fuller and deeper life with God. Jesus put it this way: "Blessed are those who hunger and thirst for righteousness, for they will be filled."

CHALLENGE

Do you have a hunger for holiness? God's desire is for you to be holy as He is holy. He'll do His part; will you do yours?

DAY 4

Trust or Worry?

I tell you, do not worry about your life, what you will eat or drink; or about your body, what you will wear. Is not life more important than food, and the body more important than clothes?
—Matthew 6:25

Did you know that some psychologists claim that 85 percent of what we worry about will never happen to us? They say there is absolutely nothing we can do about 10 percent of our worries, and that only the other 5 percent of our worries are legitimate. When you take a look at your worries in the light of these statistics, wouldn't you agree that most of your worrying is useless?

There are more people in hospital beds because of worry than almost any other disease. Headaches, ulcers, heart attacks, mental disorders, and even the common cold can be brought on by worry.

Worry is the opposite of trust, and as a Christian you are called to put your trust in God's direction for your life. One of the greatest pieces of advice ever given to humankind is from the Sermon on the Mount when Jesus said:

> Therefore I tell you, do not worry about your life, what you will eat or drink; or about your body, what you will wear. Is not life more important than food, and the body more important than clothes? Look at the birds of the air; they do not sow or reap or store away in barns, and yet your heavenly Father feeds them. Are you not much more valuable than they? Who of you by worrying can add a single hour to his life?
>
> And why do you worry about clothes? See how the lilies of the field grow. They do not labor or spin. Yet I tell you that not even Solomon in all his splendor was dressed like one of these. If that is how God clothes the grass of the field, which is here today and tomorrow is thrown into the fire, will he not much more clothe you, O you of little faith? So do not worry, saying, "What shall we eat?" or "What shall we drink?" or "What shall we wear?" For the pagans run after all these things, and your heavenly Father knows that you need them. But seek first his kingdom and his righteousness, and all these things will be given to you as well (Matthew 6:25-33).

The decision to trust God or to carry the worries of the world yourself is up to you. Either road you decide to take requires an action decision on your part. One road leads to fulfillment and peace; the other road leads to frustration and anxiety. By all means choose the road called trust! God's Word has never been proven wrong.

CHALLENGE

Do you have a problem with worry and anxiety? If you do, then make a conscious decision to place your trust and faith in the Creator of our universe, who sees beyond what our finite self can see. Which do you seek first—His kingdom or yours?

Goals for Daily Living

In his heart a man plans his course, but the
Lord determines his steps.

— Proverbs 16:9

Have you ever written down goals for living your life? I'm not talking about the do's and don'ts of legalism. I mean forming a philosophy of life and then living your life to the fullest according to your goals.

F.B. Meyer was a great writer and minister of the gospel. He had seven goals for daily living that I use and recommend.

1. Make a daily, definite consecration of yourself to God (audibly).
2. Tell God you are willing to be willing about all.
3. Reckon on Christ to do His part perfectly.
4. Confess sin instantly.
5. Hand over to Christ every temptation and care.

6. Keep in touch with Christ. (Read the Word, and good books; pray; seek places and people where He is.)
7. Expect the Holy Spirit to work in, with, and for you.

CHALLENGE

What are the goals you live by? Today write out some goals or take on F.B. Meyer's goals and pledge yourself to living by them each and every day.

DAY 6

Walking in the Light

*This is the message we have heard from him
and declare to you: God is light; in him there is
no darkness at all. If we claim to have fellowship
with him yet walk in the darkness, we lie and do
not live by the truth. But if we walk in the light,
as he is in the light, we have fellowship with one
another, and the blood of Jesus, his Son, purifies
us from all sin.*

—1 John 1:5-7

Jesus said, "I am the light of the world. Whoever follows me will never walk in darkness, but will have the light of life." The concept of light is an important concept throughout the Bible. When you walk with Jesus you walk in the light.

Light helps you to see where you are going. Without the light of God you cannot possibly know how to live your life. Living in darkness is incompatible with living in the light. If you want to walk with God you've got to stay away from the darkness and walk in the light.

In today's Scripture there are two important results of walking in the light. The first result is fellowship with one another—in other words, a right relationship with our family and friends. Secondly, when we walk in the light the blood of Jesus purifies or cleanses us from all sin, restoring a right relationship with God. When we walk in the light we have a right relationship horizontally with humankind and a right relationship vertically with God. There are no more important priorities in life.

It is interesting to note that many studies in the area of death and dying tell us that just before a person dies he seeks a right relationship with God and a right relationship with his family and friends. When all other aspects of life are put aside, the important priorities of life remain. The way to insure that your life is in proper perspective is to walk in the light.

CHALLENGE

Are there areas of darkness in your life? If so, how about shedding some *light* on them and giving them over to Christ? God's light will enable you to see where you should be going!

DAY 7

His Way or Your Way?

Jesus answered, "I am the way and the truth and the life. No one comes to the Father except through me."

—John 14:6

He is the Way. Follow Him through the Land of Unlikeness; You will see rare beasts, and have unique adventures.

He is the Truth. See Him in the Kingdom of Anxiety; You will come to a great city that has expected your return for years.

He is Life. Love Him in the World of the Flesh; And at your marriage all of its occasions shall dance for joy.*

---

* Tim Hansel, *You Gotta Keep Dancin'* (Elgin: David C. Cook, 1985), p. 131.

When we read the words of Jesus, "I am the way, the truth, and the life," sometimes we forget that He has become our substance of life. When you follow and accept His way, truth, and life, He will bring you to places and experiences beyond the normal human life. When your life is in His hands, following His call, you are on the greatest adventure that life has to offer. Nobody said it will be easy, but you can't deny that His calling in your life is the right one. Go for it—and keep your eyes fixed on Jesus so you don't lose your way!

CHALLENGE

What will it take to follow His way, obey His truth, and live His life? Don't hesitate to step out into the great adventure of His calling for your life.

8 *ATTITUDE*

DAY 1

An Attitude of Thankfulness

Give thanks in all circumstances, for this is God's will for you in Christ Jesus.
> —1 Thessalonians 5:18

There is always reason to be thankful. Notice that today's Scripture doesn't say to be thankful *for* all things but to be thankful *in* all things. Even in the most difficult of circumstances you can find reason for a thankful heart. I like the phrase that says, "I complained because I had no shoes until I met a man who had no feet." No matter what your circumstances, I believe there is a reason to be thankful in your circumstance. Your situation may never change, but your *attitude* can change, and that will make all the difference in the world.

Terry Foxe was a Canadian distance runner who started a run from one side of Canada to the other. He ran at least 26 miles a day raising money for cancer research. He was a cancer victim himself. He ran every mile on one leg, since his right leg had been amputated well above the knee. Almost every day a television announcer or radio newscaster would put a microphone in front of Terry and ask him how his run for cancer was doing. Often exhausted and losing valuable strength, Terry would say, "I don't know about tomorrow, but God gave me another day to live, and I'm thankful for each day I'm alive." Terry didn't finish his run across Canada because he died of the dreaded disease he was raising money for. Yet even to the end he remained thankful for each day and considered each day God's gift to him. With an attitude of thankfulness he made the most of a difficult situation.

CHALLENGE

How about you? Is it time to begin developing a greater attitude of thankfulness in your life? There is no better time to start than now.

Joy Is Yours

*Rejoice in the Lord always. I will say it again:
Rejoice!*

—Philippians 4:4

Did you know that over 500 times in the Bible
we are commanded to rejoice? *The Living Bible*
says, "Be full of joy." Every morning I repeat a
particular verse in the Psalms to myself. In fact
some mornings I say it while looking in the mirror,
because I don't feel joyful. Nevertheless this verse
is forever true and always helpful. Here it is:

This is the day the Lord has made;
let us rejoice and be glad in it.

—Psalm 118:24

The truth of that psalm helps me get my day
started on the right track. I have found that if I
start my day rejoicing in the Lord, my day will be
full of joy. A great preacher once said, "The surest
mark of a Christian is not faith or even love but

joy." Did you know that Jesus came to give you joy, a deep, overflowing joy that only comes from God? Jesus said, "I have told you this so that my joy may be in you and that your joy may be complete" (John 15:11).

God's kind of joy is not a giddy, superficial good feeling. Rather, His joy runs deep. Even during the tough times it prevails in your soul.

CHALLENGE

Take a moment to rejoice in the Lord. Ask to be filled with His joy. Now take His joy and give it to someone else.

Your Attitude Makes the Difference

I will bless the Lord at all times;
his praise shall continually be in my mouth.
My soul makes its boast in the Lord;
let the afflicted hear and be glad.
O magnify the Lord with me,
and let us exalt his name together!

I sought the Lord, and he answered me,
and delivered me from all my fears.
Look to him, and be radiant;
so your faces shall never be ashamed.
This poor man cried, and the Lord heard him,
and saved him out of all his troubles.

—Psalm 34:1-6 RSV

There were once two men, Mr. Wilson and Mr. Thompson, both seriously ill in the same room of a great hospital—quite a small room, just large enough for a pair of

them: two beds, two bedside lockers,
a door opening on the hall, and one
window looking out on the world.

Mr. Wilson as part of his treatment was
allowed to sit up in bed for an hour in
the afternoon (something to do with
draining the fluid from his lungs). His bed
was next to the window. But Mr. Thompson had to spend all of his time flat on
his back. Both of them had to be kept
quiet and still, which was the reason they
were in the small room themselves. They
were grateful for the peace and privacy,
though. None of the bustle and clatter
and prying eyes of the general ward for
them. Of course, one of the disadvantages
of their condition was that they weren't
allowed to do much: no reading, no radio,
certainly no television. They just had to
keep quiet and still, just the two of them.

Well, they used to talk for hours and
hours—about their wives, their children,
their homes, their jobs, their hobbies,
their childhood, what they did during the
war, where they'd been on vacations, all
that sort of thing. Every afternoon, when
Mr. Wilson, the man by the window, was
propped up for his hour, he would pass
the time by describing what he could see
outside. And Mr. Thompson began to live
for those hours.

The window apparently overlooked a

park with a lake where there were ducks
and swans, children throwing them bread
and sailing model boats, and young lovers
walking hand in hand beneath the trees.
And there were flowers and stretches of
grass, games of softball, people taking
their ease in the sunshine, and right at
the back, behind the fringe of trees, there
was a fine view of the city skyline. Mr.
Thompson would listen to all of this,
enjoying every minute—how a child
nearly fell into the lake, how beautiful
the girls were in their summer dresses,
then an exciting ball game, or a boy playing with his puppy. It got to the place
that he could almost see what was hap-
pening outside.

Then one fine afternoon when there was
some sort of parade the thought struck
him: Why should Wilson, next to the window, have all the pleasure of seeing what
was going on? Why shouldn't he get the
chance? He felt ashamed and tried not to
think like that, but the more he tried, the
worse he wanted a change. He would do
anything! In a few days he had turned
sour. *He* should be by the window. He
brooded. He couldn't sleep and grew even
more seriously ill, which the doctors just
couldn't understand.

One night as he stared at the ceiling, Mr.
Wilson suddenly woke up, coughing and
choking, the fluid congesting in his lungs,

his hands groping for the call button that would bring the night nurse running. But Mr. Thompson watched without moving. The coughing racked the darkness. On and on. He choked and then stopped. The sound of breathing stopped. Mr. Thompson continued to stare at the ceiling.

In the morning, the day nurse came in with water for their baths and found Mr. Wilson dead. They took his body away quietly, with no fuss.

As soon as it seemed decent, Mr. Thompson asked if he could be moved to the bed next to the window. So they moved him, tucked him in, made him quite comfortable, and left him alone to be quiet and still. The minute they'd gone he propped himself up on one elbow, painfully and laboriously, and strained as he looked out the window.

It faced a blank wall.*

Your attitude makes all the difference in the world. Some people face a blank wall and see dry, chipped paint while others see beautiful opportunities and numerous possibilities. How is your attitude today? In Jesus Christ you have hope. In Jesus Christ you have the knowledge that although all is not a bed of roses, God reigns and is victorious.

---

* *Ideas Books #17-20* (El Cajon: Youth Specialties, 1976), p. 151.

With the good news of Jesus your attitude can be positive, healthy, vibrant, and filled with joy.

Because of God's goodness you can look toward a bright and glorious tomorrow. You can truly say "I will bless the Lord at all times; his praise shall continually be in my mouth."

CHALLENGE

Take an attitude check today. What in your life could use a change of attitude? Read Psalm 34 again and reflect on the many things for which to be grateful in your life.

DAY 4

There Is a Season

Rejoice with those who rejoice; mourn with those who mourn.

—Romans 12:15

One of the important characteristics of a servant of God is to have the ability to rejoice with those who rejoice and weep with those who weep. Sometimes we let envy get in the way of rejoicing in other people's success. Are you the type of person who can put your own emotions and troubles aside in order to get into the feelings of your friends who need you? Jesus had the ability to celebrate with friends at a wedding party and mourn with those at the death of a loved one.

Life tends to go in circles. We must learn the meaning of these words taken from the book of Ecclesiastes:

To everything there is a season,
A time for every purpose under heaven:

A time to be born,
And a time to die;

A time to plant,
And a time to pluck what is planted...

A time to weep,
And a time to laugh...

A time to embrace,
And a time to refrain from embracing...

A time to keep silence,
And a time to speak;

A time to love,
And a time to hate;

A time of war,
And a time of peace.
                    —Ecclesiastes 3:1-8 NKJV

When you learn this truth you'll learn one of the most important lessons of life: To everything there is a season, and a time to every purpose under heaven.

CHALLENGE

How are you at rolling with the seasons of life? Do you have the ability to weep with those who weep and rejoice with those who rejoice? Resolve today to make this characteristic a stronger part of your life.

Thankful People Are Happy People

Give thanks to the God of heaven. His love endures forever.

—Psalm 136:26

A few years ago a woman was standing on top of a 54-story building in New York City. She was ready to jump to her death, and the police suicide squad was taking her extremely seriously. She didn't look the type in her expensive dress and distinguished appearance, but regardless of her appearance every attempt to convince her to get down from the ledge ended in failure. One of the police officers called his pastor to pray. His pastor said he would come right over and see if he could help. When this wise minister appraised the situation he asked the captain if he might try to get close enough to talk with the woman. The captain shrugged and said, "What do we have to lose?"

The pastor started walking toward her, but she screamed as before, "Don't come any closer or I'll jump!" He took a step backward and called out to

her, "I'm sorry you believe no one loves you!"
This got her attention and also the attention of the
suicide squad because it was so unorthodox. The
pastor went on to say, "Your grandchildren must
never have given you any attention." At this statement she took a step toward him and emphatically
replied, "My family loves me and my grandchildren are wonderful—I have eight grandchildren."
The pastor took a step toward her and said, "But
you must be very poor to be so desperate to
jump." She looked at her plump body and very
nice dress and said, "Do I look like I'm in need of
a meal? We live in Central Park in a beautiful
apartment." The pastor took another step and was
now within three feet of her. He asked, "Then
why do you want to jump and kill yourself?" Her
surprising reply was, "I don't remember."

This pastor had helped turn her focus off her
problems and on to reasons to be thankful. They
continued to talk while she showed him pictures of
her eight grandchildren with lengthy descriptions
of each family member! A year later she was a
volunteer on a suicide prevention hotline, helping
people to choose life and choose the thankful life.
She had learned the secret that thankful people are
happy people.

CHALLENGE

Make today a day filled with thanksgiving. Start
with a few minutes of giving thanks to God, and
then tell your friends and family why you are
thankful. When you're thankful you'll wear a
smile!

DAY 6

Garbage In,
Garbage Out

Whatever is true, whatever is noble, whatever is right, whatever is pure, whatever is lovely, whatever is admirable—if anything is excellent or praiseworthy—think about such things.
—Philippians 4:8

There's a simple principle that says when you put garbage into your mind and life, garbage will come out. When you put good things into your mind and life, then good things will flow out. Your mind matters, and what you put into your mind will ultimately make the difference between peace or distraction.

Today take a few minutes to take the advice of Paul and think about what is true, noble, right, pure, lovely, admirable, excellent, and praiseworthy. God's promise to you in verse 9 is that when you think of these things the "God of peace will be with you."

People of peace are people who have learned with God's help to control their mind. They regulate what goes in, and peace prevails. Others choose to put garbage into their mind, and garbage naturally comes out.

Your mind is a powerful source of help and positive energy. Give your mind and thoughts over to God's power and you'll begin to think the thoughts of our Lord and live with the peace from above. Don't waste your precious life with less than what God has to offer. Heed this advice from Romans 12:2:

> Do not conform any longer to the pattern of this world, but be transformed by the renewing of your mind. Then you will be able to test and approve what God's will is—his good, pleasing and perfect will.

CHALLENGE

How can you apply Philippians 4:8 and Romans 12:2 to your life today? Make a plan for the area you need to work on, and ask God for His help as you claim His promise for peace in your soul.

Count Your Blessings

Know that the Lord is God. It is he who made us, and we are his; we are his people, the sheep of his pasture. Enter his gates with thanksgiving and his courts with praise; give thanks to him and praise his name. For the Lord is good and his love endures forever; his faithfulness continues through all generations.

—Psalm 100:3-5

Sometimes we get so preoccupied with our problems and struggles that we forget to count our blessings. Sometimes we have to get outside ourselves and remember to ask questions such as, "What would a blind person give to see the pleasant rivers, meadows, and flowers that I enjoy daily?"

Today look at the world through the eyes of a person who has received great blessings from God. As you look upon your blessings, pause to give God praise for His mighty works. When I'm feeling low I often take a few minutes to jot down in my journal or on a piece of paper at least 20 blessings from God. My attitude always changes when I remember to count my blessings!

CHALLENGE

Sometime today literally count your blessings. Take out a sheet of paper and write out at least 20 blessings in your life. I guarantee that it will change your perspective on your day!

DAY 1

Radical Commitment

Jesus replied: "Love the Lord your God with all your heart and with all your soul and with all your mind." This is the first and greatest commandment. And the second is like it: "Love your neighbor as yourself." All the Law and the Prophets hang on these two commandments.
                                    —Matthew 22:37-40

Our love for God goes beyond lip service or sitting in the pew on Sunday. God wants all that we have and all that we are to become His. Sometimes the actions of people of other faiths or causes puts my actions to shame. The following letter is written by a Communist student who broke off his engagement with his fiancee. While you read this letter, think how it compares to your commitment and dedication to Jesus Christ.

> We communists have a high casualty rate. We are the ones who get shot and hung and ridiculed and fired from our jobs and in every other way made as

uncomfortable as possible. A certain percentage of us get killed or imprisoned. We live in virtual poverty. We turn back to the party every penny we make above what is absolutely necessary to keep us alive. We communists do not have the time or the money for many movies, or concerts, or T-bone steaks, or decent homes, or new cars. We have been described as fanatics. We are fanatics. Our lives are dominated by one great overshadowing factor: the struggle for world communism. We communists have a philosophy of life which no amount of money can buy. We have a cause to fight for, a definite purpose in life. We subordinate our petty personal selves into the great movement of humanity; and if our personal lives seem hard or our egos appear to suffer through subordination to the party, then we are adequately compensated by the thought that each of us in his small way is contributing to something new and true and better for mankind. There is one thing in which I am dead earnest about, and that is the communist cause. It is my life, my business, my religion, my hobby, my sweetheart, my wife, and my mistress, my breath and meat. I work at it in the daytime and dream of it at night. Its hold on me grows, not lessens, as time goes on; therefore, I cannot carry on a friendship, a love affair, or even a conversation without relating it to this force which both

drives and guides my life. I evaluate
people, books, ideas, and actions according to how they affect the communist
cause, and by their attitude toward it. I've
already been in jail because of my ideals,
and if necessary, I'm ready to go before a
firing squad.*

CHALLENGE

Can you speak similar words about your commitment to Jesus as the Communist student did about
his faith in the Communist cause? What does it
mean for you to love God with your whole heart,
mind, and soul?

* Bill Bright, *Revolution Now* (San Bernardino:
Campus Crusade for Christ, 1969), pp. 186-87.

DAY 2

A Full Surrender

I urge you, brothers, in view of God's mercy, to offer your bodies as living sacrifices, holy and pleasing to God—which is your spiritual worship. Do not conform any longer to the pattern of this world, but be transformed by the renewing of your mind. Then you will be able to test and approve what God's will is—his good, pleasing and perfect will.

—Romans 12:1,2

I would love to buy $3 worth of God, please, not enough to explode my soul or disturb my sleep, but just enough to equal a cup of warm milk or a snooze in the sunshine. I don't want enough of Him to make me love a black man or pick beets with a migrant. I want ecstasy, not transformation; I want the warmth of the womb, not a new birth. I want a pound of the Eternal in a paper sack. I would like to buy $3 worth of God, please.*

---

* Charles Swindoll, *Improving Your Serve* (Waco: Word, 1981), p. 28.

I'm afraid too many people approach their Christian faith as if they wanted to buy three dollars' worth of God. They want only the best that God has to offer. As today's Scripture points out, you can't have both. God's desire for your life is that you actually give your body as a living sacrifice to Him. If you choose to identify with Jesus you are choosing to make Him the Master of your life. A fully surrendered life to Jesus is living on the edge of adventure.

CHALLENGE

Are there certain areas of your life that you have not surrendered to God? Maybe it's your finances or a personal relationship or even an area of your spiritual discipline. Now is the time to give it all to Jesus!

DAY 3

Overcommitment and Fatigue: A Deadly Sin

They who wait for the Lord shall renew their strength, they shall mount up with wings like eagles, they shall run and not be weary, they shall walk and not faint.

—Isaiah 40:31 RSV

We live in a culture which has often fooled us into believing that more is better and busyness is a virtue. Far too many people in our world are spiritually, emotionally, and physically bankrupt because they are overcommitted and fatigued. Vince Lombardi said, "Fatigue makes cowards of us all." The comedian Flip Wilson summed it up best for many of us when he said, "If I had my entire life to live over again, I doubt if I'd have the strength."

I don't believe that God wants us to be one step from a nervous breakdown, always on the edge of exhaustion. What's the answer? There are no easy formulas for success, but there are two suggestions that I want you to think about today.

1. Cut back and do less.

If this means making less money, cutting back on your social obligations, or even taking a night off from church activities, then do whatever it takes to not be so overcommitted and fatigued. A friend of mine once told me, "If the devil can't make you bad, he'll make you busy."

2. Rest.

Rest should be a nonnegotiable time in everyone's life. Even God rested! Exodus 31:17 says, "In six days the Lord made heaven and earth, and on the seventh day he rested and was refreshed" (RSV). When we rest we get a proper perspective on our life. When we rest we can reflect on what has taken place in our life during the week. Does your life have control of you, or do you have control of your life? Rest and reflection will help you answer that important question.

CHALLENGE

Today take an evaluation of your fatigue and overcommitment level. If you are spiritually, emotionally, or physically bankrupt, then it's time to cut back, do less, and rest. What is the next day you have scheduled to relax?

DAY 4

Try It . . . You'll Like It!

O taste and see that the Lord is good!
Happy is the man who takes refuge in him!
                              —Psalm 34:8 RSV

One of my favorite storytellers is Dr. Anthony Campolo. I love how he tells the story of Blondin, the tightrope-walker who in the 1890's strung a tightrope across the Niagara Falls.

> Before ten thousand screaming people [he] inched his way from the Canadian side of the falls to the United States side. When he got there the crowd began shouting his name: "Blondin! Blondin! Blondin! Blondin!"

> Finally he raised his arms, quieted the crowd, and [how's this for an ego trip?] shouted to them, "I am Blondin! Do you believe in me?" The crowd shouted back, "We believe! We believe! We believe!"

Again he quieted the crowd, and once more he shouted to them, "I'm going back across the tightrope, but this time I'm going to carry someone on my back. Do you believe I can do that?" The crowd yelled, "We believe! We believe!"

He quieted them one more time, and then he said, "Who will be that person?" The crowd went dead. Nothing.

Finally, out of the crowd stepped one man. He climbed on Blondin's shoulders, and for the next three-and-a-half-hours, Blondin inched his way back across the tightrope to the Canadian side of the falls.

The point of the story is blatantly clear: Ten thousand people stood there that day chanting, "We believe, we believe!" but only one person really believed. Believing is not just saying, "I accept the fact." Believing is giving your life over into the hands of the one in whom you say you believe.*

Christ calls you to step out of your comfort zone and walk with Him. Stepping out on faith means that you don't know all that is going to happen but you are putting your trust in Someone who does. Putting your trust with Jesus is not always the comfortable way to go. The risk you take is that God knows what He is doing better than you know

---

* Tony Campolo, *You Can Make a Difference* (Waco: Word, 1984), p. 14.

what you are doing. History and common sense tell me to put my faith in the infinite Creator and Savior of the universe rather than in unstable me. Are you ready to take another step in the direction of faith? Then accept God's challenge to "taste and see"!

CHALLENGE

What are you doing right now in your life that could not be done without the supernatural power of Christ? Those who live their lives in touch with Jesus are not afraid to step out of their comfort zone and into the realm of faith.

DAY 5

We Are an Offering

*Commit your way to the Lord; trust in him,
and he will act.*

—Psalm 37:5 RSV

On many a Sunday morning at our church we
sing a song titled "We Are an Offering." It deeply
expresses my desire to be God's person. Here is
what the song says:

> We lift our voices, we lift our hands;
> We lift our lives up to You, we are an
>   offering.
> Lord, use our voices, Lord, use our hands,
> Lord, use our lives—they are Yours, we
>   are an offering.
>
> All that we are, all that we have,
> All that we hope to be we give to You,
>   we give to You.*

---

* "We Are an Offering," Dwight Liles Bug & Bear
Music, Home Sweet Home Records Inc., 1984.

Paul challenged the Christians in Rome, "In view of God's mercy...offer your bodies as living sacrifices, holy and pleasing to God—which is your spiritual worship." Jesus was an offering on the cross for our salvation. Our lives in return must be a living offering to our Lord and Savior Jesus Christ.

CHALLENGE

Do you view your life as an offering to God? Today pray the prayer in the song above: "Lord, use my voice, Lord, use my hands, Lord, use my life."

DAY 6

No More Excuses

Some time later, Jesus went up to Jerusalem for a feast of the Jews. Now there is in Jerusalem near the Sheep Gate a pool, which in Aramaic is called Bethesda and which is surrounded by five covered colonnades. Here a great number of disabled people used to lie—the blind, the lame, the paralyzed. One who was there had been an invalid for thirty-eight years. When Jesus saw him lying there and learned that he had been in this condition for a long time, he asked him, "Do you want to get well?"

"Sir," the invalid replied, "I have no one to help me into the pool when the water is stirred. While I am trying to get in, someone else goes down ahead of me."

Then Jesus said to him, "Get up! Pick up your mat and walk."

—John 5:1-8

I'm convinced that procrastination should be added to the seven deadly sins in the book of Proverbs. There is a great tendency among us human beings to put off making commitments and living life to the fullest. The excuses are abysmal:

"When I get out of school, then I'll commit my life to God." "When I get married, then my life will be happy." "As soon as I have some money, my life will change."

In today's Scripture we meet a man who had been sick for 38 years. Jesus asked him the big question: "Do you want to get well?" Notice that he didn't answer the question with an immediate yes, but hesitated and made an excuse. At times we are so much like the sick man: We know what God wants us to do, but we pause and make an excuse.

One morning a vulture was hungry. While flying over the river, he saw a dead animal's carcass floating down the river on a piece of ice. The vulture landed on the ice and began to gorge himself with this delightful meal. He looked up to take a breath of air and noticed that he was 100 yards from a waterfall and that the ice was moving rapidly toward the waterfall. But instead of flying away, he kept eating, though keeping his eye on the waterfall. At 25 yards he decided to take one last bite. Then at 10 yards he took one last mouthful. With only a few feet to go before the falls he tried to fly, but his feet were now frozen to the ice, and he tumbled to his death over the falls.

Don't make excuses! Many a person has wasted his life by putting off the vital long-term priorities for the less important short-term ones.

CHALLENGE

Is there something in your life that you have been putting off with a feeble excuse? Make a commitment *now*.

DAY 7

Taking a Stand

The man who loves his life will lose it, while the man who hates his life in this world will keep it for eternal life. Whoever serves me must follow me; and where I am, my servant also will be. My Father will honor the one who serves me.
—John 12:25,26

Today's story shows how one insignificant person can make a difference in the history of the world. All it takes is faith and a single-minded belief that you are one of Christ's healing agents to a lonely and hurting world.

In the fourth century there lived an Asiatic monk who had spent most of his life in a remote prayer community, raising vegetables for the cloister kitchen. When he was not tending his garden spot, he was fulfilling his vocation of study and prayer.

Then one day this monk, named Telemachus, felt that the Lord wanted him to

163

go to Rome, the capital of the world—the busiest, wealthiest, biggest city in the world. Telemachus had no idea why he should go there, and he was terrified at the thought. But as he prayed, God's directive became clear.

How bewildered the little monk must have been as he set out on the long journey, on foot, over dusty roads westward, everything he owned on his back! Why was he going? He didn't know. What would he find there? He had no idea. But obediently, he went.

Telemachus arrived in Rome during the holiday festival. You may know that the Roman rulers kept the ghettos quiet in those days by providing free bread and special entertainment called circuses. At the time Telemachus arrived the city was also bustling with excitement over the recent Roman victory over the Goths. In the midst of this jubilant commotion, the monk looked for clues as to why God had brought him there, for he had no guidance, not even a superior in a religious order to contact.

Perhaps, he thought, it is not sheer coincidence that I have arrived at this festival time. Perhaps God has some special role for me to play.

So Telemachus let the crowds guide him, and the stream of humanity soon led him into the Coliseum, where the gladiator contests were to be staged. He could hear the cries of the animals in their cages beneath the floor of the great arena and the clamor of the contestants preparing to do battle.

The gladiators marched into the arena, saluted the emperor, and shouted, "We who are about to die salute thee." Telemachus shuddered. He had never heard of gladiator games before, but had a premonition of awful violence.

The crowd had come to cheer men who, for no reason other than amusement, would murder each other. Human lives were offered for entertainment. As the monk realized what was going to happen, he realized he could not sit still and watch such savagery. Neither could he leave and forget. He jumped to the top of the perimeter wall and cried, "In the name of Christ, forbear!"

The fighting began, of course. No one paid the slightest heed to the puny voice. So Telemachus pattered down the stone steps and leapt onto the sandy floor of the arena. He made a comic figure—a scrawny man in a monk's habit dashing back and forth between muscular, armed athletes. One gladiator sent him sprawling with a blow from his shield, directing him back to his seat. It was a rough gesture, though almost a kind one. The crowd roared.

But Telemachus refused to stop. He rushed into the way of those trying to fight, shouting again, "In the name of Christ, forbear!" The crowd began to laugh and cheer him on, perhaps thinking him part of the entertainment.

Then his movement blocked the vision of one of the contestants; the gladiator saw a blow coming just in time. Furious now, the crowd began to cry for the interloper's blood.

"Run him through!" they screamed.

The gladiator he had blocked raised his sword and with a flash of steel struck Telemachus, slashing down across his chest and into his stomach. The little monk gasped once more, "In the name of Christ, forbear."

Then a strange thing occurred. As the two gladiators and the crowd focused on the still form on the suddenly crimson sand, the arena fell deathly quiet. In the silence, someone in the top tier got up and walked out. Another followed. All over the arena, spectators began to leave, until the huge stadium was emptied.

There were other forces at work, of course, but that innocent figure lying in the pool of blood crystallized the

opposition, and that was the last gladi-
atorial contest in the Roman Coliseum.
Never again did men kill each other for
the crowds' entertainment in the Roman
arena.*

CHALLENGE

Has God placed a cause worth fighting for in
your life? Maybe it is time for you to take a stand
on the side of justice.

* Charles Colson, *Loving God*, (Grand Rapids:
Zondervan, 1983), pp. 241-43. Used by permission.

Love Is the Great Transformer

These three things remain: faith, hope and love. But the greatest of these is love.
—1 Corinthians 13:13

Paul wrote to his fellow Christians in Corinth, "No eye has seen, no ear has heard, no mind has conceived what God has prepared for those who love him" (1 Corinthians 2:9). There is no one in this world who can be in love with God and remain the same. Someone sent me a card that said,

LOVE is the Great Transformer...LOVE transforms:

Ambition into aspiration,
Greed into gratitude,
Selfishness into service,
Getting into giving,
Demands into dedication,
Loneliness into happiness.

Love transforms you into becoming a person with more of the qualities of Jesus Christ. Dedicate your life to love. Don't let our culture cheapen the meaning and transformation that takes place with agape love, God's highest form of love. When you seek the higher level of love you can rest assured that your life will never be the same.

CHALLENGE

What area of your life could use some transformation through love? How has the love of God shaped your life in a more positive direction?

DAY 2

God Loves You Just the Way You Are

We love because he first loved us.
                              —1 John 4:19

Once upon a time there was a young girl named Susie. She was a beautiful little girl with the most wonderful doll collection in the world. Her father traveled all over the world on business, and for nearly 12 years he had brought dolls home to Susie. In her bedroom she had shelves of dolls from all over the United States and from every other continent on earth. She had dolls that could sing and dance and do just about anything a doll could possibly do.

One day one of her father's business acquaintances came to visit. At dinner he asked Susie about her wonderful doll collection. After dinner Susie took him by the hand and showed him these marvelous dolls from all over the world. He was very impressed. After he took the "grand tour" and was introduced to many of the beautiful dolls, he asked Susie, "With all these precious dolls you must have one that is your favorite. Which one is it?"

Without a moment's hesitation Susie went over to her old beat-up toy box and started pulling out toys. From the bottom of the box she pulled out one of the most ragged dolls you have ever seen. There were only a few strands of hair left on the head. The clothing had long since disappeared. The doll was filthy from many years of play outside. One of the buttons for the eyes was hanging down, with only a string to keep it connected. Stuffing was coming out at the elbow and knee. Susie handed the doll to the gentleman and said, "This doll is my favorite."

The man was shocked and asked, "Why is this doll with all these beautiful dolls in your room?"

She replied, "If I didn't love this doll, nobody would!"

That single statement moved the businessman to tears. It was such a simple statement, yet so profound. The little girl loved her doll unconditionally. She loved the doll not for its beauty or abilities but simply because it was her very own doll.*

* Jim Burns, *Handling Your Hormones: The Straight Scoop on Love and Sexuality* (Eugene: Harvest House, 1986), pp. 46-47.

God loves you the way Susie loved her doll. God loves you not for what you do but for who you are. You never need to earn God's love. He loves you because you are His special creation because of God's unconditional love you are free to blossom into all He wants you to be. His love has no strings attached.

CHALLENGE

How do you feel when you comprehend God's unconditional love for you? Take a moment to offer Him your praise and thanksgiving for His gracious, never-ending, never-fading love for you.

DAY 3

Spread Your Love Around

If I speak in the tongues of men and of angels, but have not love, I am only a resounding gong or a clanging cymbal. If I have the gift of prophecy and can fathom all mysteries and all knowledge, and if I have a faith that can move mountains, but have not love, I am nothing. If I give all I possess to the poor and surrender my body to the flames, but have not love, I gain nothing.
          —1 Corinthians 13:1-3

Sometimes I feel like I can't do much to serve God or help my family and friends. But about the time I feel helpless, God reminds me that the greatest gift I can give to other people is me! People respond to love. People respond to sharing your life with them. Today I want to offer you a beautiful thought about sharing.

> There isn't much that I can do, but I can share my bread with you, and sometimes share a sorrow, too—as on our way we go.

There isn't much that I can do, but I can sit
an hour with you, and I can share a joke with
you, and sometimes share reverses, too—as on
our way we go.

There isn't much that I can do, but I can share
my flowers with you, and I can share my
books with you, and sometimes share your
burdens, too—as on our way we go.

There isn't much that I can do, but I can share
my songs with you, and I can share my mirth
with you, and sometimes come and laugh with
you—as on our way we go.

There isn't much that I can do, but I can share
my hopes with you, and I can share my fears
with you, and sometimes shed some tears with
you—as on our way we go.

There isn't much that I can do, but I can share
my friends with you, and I can share my life
with you, and oftentimes share a prayer with
you—as on our way we go.*

CHALLENGE

Who can you share your life with today? What
specific practical things can you do for them to let
them know you care? For starters, tell someone
today that you love him.

---

* Tim Hansel, *You Gotta Keep Dancin'*
(Elgin: David C. Cook, 1985), pp. 16-17.

Love Makes the Difference

A new commandment I give you: Love one another. As I have loved you, so you must love one another. All men will know that you are my disciples if you love one another.

—John 13:34,35

As you look at today's Scripture, think of it in this way: The non-Christian world has the right to judge whether there is a God or not a God by the way we Christians love each other.

Yes, the world will know us by our fruit. There is no greater witness of God's love on earth than when Christians love in the same manner as Jesus loves.

Here is how historian Aristides described the Christians to the Roman Emperor Hadrian:

They love one another. They never fail to help widows; they save orphans from those who would hurt them. If they have something, they give freely to the man who has nothing; if they see a stranger, they take him home, and are happy, as though he were a real brother. They don't consider themselves brothers in the usual sense, but brothers instead through the Spirit, in God.*

Aristides was describing the kingdom of God made visible by believers. One of the major duties of every Christian is to make the invisible kingdom of God visible.

CHALLENGE

If you were arrested for being a Christian, would there be enough evidence to convict you? One of the major factors to take into consideration would be your manner of love.

---

* Charles Colson, *Loving God* (Grand Rapids: Zondervan, 1983), p. 176.

DAY 5

The Law of Love

You have heard that it was said, "Love your neighbor and hate your enemy." But I tell you: Love your enemies and pray for those who persecute you, that you may be sons of your Father in heaven. He causes his sun to rise on the evil and the good, and sends rain on the righteous and the unrighteous. If you love those who love you, what reward will you get? Are not even the tax collectors doing that? And if you greet only your brothers, what are you doing more than others? Do not even pagans do that?

—Matthew 5:43-47

When you choose to follow Jesus Christ you are choosing to do things His way. He wants you to love people with His love, and this kind of love goes so far as to love even our enemies.

One of the most influential stories in my life happened during World War I. The story was told by an old colonel in the Austrian Army.

I was commanded to march against a
little town on the Tyrol and lay siege to
it. We had been meeting stubborn resistance in that part of the country, but we
felt sure that we should win because all
of the advantages were on our side. My
confidence, however, was arrested by a
remark from a prisoner we had taken.
"You will never take that town," he said,
"for they have an invincible leader."

"What does the fellow mean?" I inquired
of one of my staff. "And who is this
leader of whom he speaks?"

Nobody seemed able to answer my question, and so in case there should be
some truth in the report, I doubled
preparations.

As we descended through the pass in the
Alps, I saw with surprise that the cattle
were still grazing in the valley and that
women and children—yes, and even
men—were working in the fields.

"Either they are not expecting us, or this
is a trap to catch us," I thought to myself.
As we drew nearer the town we passed
people on the road. They smiled and
greeted us with a friendly word, and then
went on their way.

Finally we reached the town and clattered
up the cobble-paved streets—colors flying,

horns sounding a challenge, arms in readiness. Women came to the windows or doorways with little babies in their arms. Some of them looked startled and held the babies closer, then went quietly on with their household tasks without panic or confusion. It was impossible to keep strict discipline, and I began to feel rather foolish. My soldiers answered the questions of children, and I saw one old warrior throw a kiss to a little golden-haired tot on a doorstep. "Just the size of Lisa," he muttered. Still no sign of an ambush. We rode straight to the open square which faced the town hall. Here, if anywhere, resistance surely was to be expected.

Just as I had reached the hall and my guard was drawn up at attention, an old white-haired man, who by his insignia I surmised to be the mayor, stepped forth, followed by ten men in simple peasant costume. They were all dignified and unabashed by the armed force before them—the most terrible soldiers of the great and mighty army of Austria.

He walked down the steps straight to my horse's side, and with hand extended, cried, "Welcome, brother!" One of my aides made a gesture as if to strike him down with his sword, but I saw by the face of the old mayor that this was no trick on his part.

"Where are your soldiers?" I demanded.

"Soldiers? Why, don't you know we have none?" he replied in wonderment, as though I had asked, "Where are your giants?" or "Where are your dwarfs?"

"But we have come to take this town."

"Well, no one will stop you."

"Are there none here to fight?"

At this question, the old man's face lit up with a rare smile that I will always remember. Often afterward, when engaged in bloody warfare, I would suddenly see that man's smile—and somehow, I came to hate my business. His words were simply:

"No, there is no one here to fight. We have chosen Christ for our Leader, and He taught men another way."*

CHALLENGE

Is there someone who has done you wrong? Is it possible for you to pray for him and try to love him? The world offers bitterness, but you have chosen Christ as your Leader, and He has taught you another way.

---

* Clarence Jordan, *Sermon on the Mount* (Valley Forge: Judson Press, 1970), pp. 59-60.

DAY 6

Amazing Grace

It is by grace you have been saved, through
faith—and this not from yourselves, it is the gift
of God—not by works, so that no one can boast.
—Ephesians 2:8,9

John Newton was a slave-trader and a free-thinker. He lived his life opposite to what would be honoring to God. He was described as a man whose curses and lifestyle expressed his revulsion against the very idea of God's existence.

One day out at sea the slave-trading boat that Newton was on began to break apart in an incredibly furious storm. Something snapped in Newton's mind, and he remembered a verse of Scripture he had heard as a child:

> If ye then, being evil, know how to give
> good gifts unto your children, how much
> more shall your Father which is in
> heaven give good things to them that ask
> him?
> —Matthew 7:11 KJV

"God, if this is true," Newton prayed earnestly, "make good Your Word. Cleanse my vile heart."

Four weeks later, in April 1748, the ship limped into an Irish harbor. Newton went to church and professed Jesus Christ was his Lord and Savior.

The song that best expresses his redemption is one of the most popular songs ever sung in the Christian faith:

> Amazing grace! How sweet the sound
> That saved a wretch like me!
> I once was lost, but now am found,
> Was blind, but now I see.
>
> 'Twas grace that taught my heart to fear,
> And grace my fears relieved;
> How precious did that grace appear
> The hour I first believed!
>
> Through many dangers, toils, and snares
> I have already come;
> It's grace that brought me safe thus far,
> And grace will lead me home.
>
> When we've been there ten thousand years
> Bright shining as the sun,
> We've no less days to sing God's praise
> Than when we've first begun.

CHALLENGE

Can you read the words of the song "Amazing Grace" and say, "I have also experienced Amazing Grace"? The grace of God means that His undeserved favor has been given to you and that your sins are forever forgiven.

DAY 7

Sacrificial Love

God demonstrates his own love for us in this:
While we were still sinners, Christ died for us.
—Romans 5:8

God's love is a sacrificial love. The famous statement of Jesus found in John 3:16 expresses this love best:

> God so loved the world that he gave his one and only Son, that whoever believes in him shall not perish but have eternal life.

God allowed His only Son to suffer and die in order for you to experience an abundant life on earth and eternal life with God.

When I look at the cross I am reminded of the ultimate sacrifice that Jesus Christ made to demonstrate His love for me. His love was not just words; it was a sacrificial deed with eternal consequences. I'm convinced that if you were the only person who needed the redemption of God, Jesus would still have gone to the cross just for you.

What is our proper response to this sacrificial love? We humble ourselves, make Christ our Lord, and daily give Him our praise and thanksgiving for His mighty sacrifice. We never have to love God out of responsibility; instead, we love Him simply out of response for what He has done for us. Next time you notice a cross, pause and offer your sincere thanks for His ultimate sacrifice of love.

CHALLENGE

Sometime today read about the physical pain and suffering that Christ went through when He died for you. Often we need to be reminded of His sacrifice so that we might have life. Our response to His sacrifice should always involve our gratitude.

CHAPTER 11

CHRISTIAN ADVENTURE

DAY 1

Authentic Christianity

We loved you so much that we were delighted to share with you not only the gospel of God but our lives as well, because you had become so dear to us.

—1 Thessalonians 2:8

Be authentic. Be yourself. There is no greater witness than a person who is open and vulnerable about his love for God and his struggles. I don't know about you, but I can't relate to perfect people. Yet there are loads of Christians running around today who want you to think they are perfect. People who act like they don't have problems are one of the major stumbling blocks to their friends and family becoming Christians. I like the bumper sticker that says, "Christians aren't perfect—they're just forgiven."

I think the old skin horse gave the Velveteen Rabbit some outstanding advice about being an authentic person. Maybe this advice is good for you as well.

The Skin Horse had lived longer in the nursery than any of the others. He was so old that his brown coat was bald in patches and showed the seams underneath, and most of the hairs on his tail had been pulled out to string bead necklaces. He was wise, for he had seen a long succession of mechanical toys arrive to boast and swagger, and by-and-by break their mainsprings and pass away, and he knew that they were only toys, and would never turn into anything else. For nursery magic is very strange and wonderful, and only those playthings that are old and wise and experienced like the Skin Horse understand all about it.

"What is REAL?" asked the Rabbit one day, when they were lying side by side near the nursery fender, before Nana came to tidy the room. "Does it mean having things that buzz inside you and a stick-out handle?"

"Real isn't how you are made," said the Skin Horse. "It's a thing that happens to you. When a child loves you for a long, long time, not just to play with, but REALLY loves you, then you become Real."

"Does it hurt?" asked the Rabbit.

"Sometimes," said the Skin Horse, for he was always truthful. "When you are Real you don't mind being hurt."

"Does it happen all at once, like being wound up," he asked, "or bit by bit?"

"It doesn't happen all at once," said the Skin Horse. "You become. It takes a long time. That's why it doesn't often happen to people who break easily, or have sharp edges, or who have to be carefully kept. Generally, by the time you are Real, most of your hair has been loved off, and your eyes drop out and you get loose in the joints and very shabby. But these things don't matter at all, because once you are Real you can't be ugly, except to people who don't understand."*

CHALLENGE

Don't pretend to be someone you're not. If you have some hurts, doubts, or struggles talk to someone about them. Don't strive to act perfect, but strive to be more like Jesus. Like the Skin Horse, an authentic Christian lifestyle takes time.

---

* Margery Williams, *The Velveteen Rabbit* (New York: Avon Books, 1975), pp. 16-17.

Wasted Hours or Invested Hours?

Give ear to my words, O Lord;
give heed to my groaning.
Hearken to the sound of my cry,
my King and my God,
for to thee do I pray.
O Lord, in the morning thou dost hear my voice;
in the morning I prepare a sacrifice for thee, and
watch.

—Psalm 5:1-3 RSV

I'm the type of person who feels if I'm not doing something I'm wasting my time. Prayer has been difficult for me at times because I feel it is getting in the way of me accomplishing something for the day. How wrong I am when I have this attitude! Prayer is not wasted hours but *invested* hours. Out of solitude comes strength...out of quiet comes peace...out of talking and listening to the Lord comes vision.

This poem is a helpful reminder of what I am talking about.

I wasted an hour one morning beside a
mountain stream,

I seized a cloud from the sky above and
fashioned myself a dream.

In the hush of the early twilight, far from
the haunts of men,

I wasted a summer evening, and fashioned my dream again.

Wasted? Perhaps. Folks say so who never
have walked with God,

When lanes are purple with lilacs or
yellow with goldenrod.

But I have found strength for my labors
in that one short evening hour.

I have found joy and contentment; I have
found peace and power.

My dreaming has left me a treasure, a
hope that is strong and true.

From wasted hours I have built my life
and found my faith anew.

—Author Unknown

CHALLENGE

Do you have a daily quiet time? Have you set
aside periodic extended times to rebuild your
relationship with God? If not, the wisest decision
you could make this week is to commit to a quiet
time with God.

DAY 3

Be Authentic

Do not merely listen to the word, and so deceive yourselves. Do what it says. Anyone who listens to the word but does not do what it says is like a man who looks at his face in a mirror and, after looking at himself, goes away and immediately forgets what he looks like. But the man who looks intently into the perfect law that gives freedom, and continues to do this, not forgetting what he has heard, but doing it—he will be blessed in what he does.

—James 1:22-25

To make a difference in your world you've got to be real. There is nothing worse than a holier-than-thou Christian who never shares his hurts and sorrows. I don't know about you, but I can't relate to perfection. Authentic people make a difference in the world. I heard recently of a minister in the Midwest who was going for a walk with a soap salesman in the community who was a real skeptic toward Christianity. They were having quite an active debate while walking through the park. The businessman was getting in some good jabs at the inconsistency of Christians. As they were walking through the park the soap salesman questioned the minister, "How can you say that Christianity works when even within the inner-city park you see derelicts of every kind, drugs, and prostitutes? Then you have the problems of the family, war, and disease, not to mention the negative problems of the world. How can you say that Christianity works? Just look around—it's not working." They walked in silence for a few moments, and then the minister turned to him and said, "You're a soap salesman, right?" "Yes, of course," was the reply. "Is it good soap?" "It's the best soap on the market!" was the comment of the salesman. The minister turned and pointed to a small child playing in the park who was covered with dirt and grime, and said, "This boy is dirty and filthy from the mud in the park; doesn't your soap help him?" The salesman said, "Well, you've got to apply the soap." The minister's response was, "So it is with the Christian faith. You must *apply* the Christian faith in order for it to work."

CHALLENGE

Make sure your *walk* is as strong as your *talk*. In what area of your life do you need to be more authentic? You must apply the Christian faith in order to make it work.

Fellowship: A Necessary Ingredient

Let us consider how we may spur one another on toward love and good deeds. Let us not give up meeting together, as some are in the habit of doing, but let us encourage one another—and all the more as you see the Day approaching.
                                                    —Hebrews 10:24,25

The Bible calls the church "the bride of Christ." God loves the church even with all of her inconsistencies. I honestly believe that you cannot be all God intends you to be without experiencing the intimate fellowship which the church has to offer. The church is not a place for you to come, sit, and be entertained. You are a part of the church. You have a job.

The church is like a lifesaving station, and this story helps me get a better perspective of what the church of Jesus Christ is all about and what my role in the church should be.

On a dangerous sea coast where shipwrecks often occur there was once a
crude little lifesaving station. The building
was just a hut, and there was only one
boat, but the few devoted members kept
a constant watch over the sea, and with
no thought for themselves went out day
and night tirelessly searching for the lost.
Some of those who were saved, and various others in the surrounding area,
wanted to become associated with the station and give of their time and money
and effort for the support of its work.
New boats were bought and new crews
trained. The little lifesaving station grew.

Some of the members of the lifesaving
station were unhappy that the building
was so crude and poorly equipped. They
felt that a more comfortable place should
be provided as the first refuge of those
saved from the sea. They replaced the
emergency cots with beds and put better
furniture in the enlarged building. Now
the lifesaving station became a popular
gathering place for its members, and they
decorated it beautifully and furnished it
exquisitely, because they used it as a
sort of club. Fewer members were now
interested in going to sea on lifesaving
missions, so they hired lifeboat crews to
do this work. The lifesaving motif still
prevailed in this club's decoration, and
there was a liturgical lifeboat in the room
where the club initiations were held.

About this time a large ship was wrecked off the coast, and the hired crews brought in boatloads of cold, wet, and half-drowned people. They were dirty and sick, and some of them had black skin and some had yellow skin. The beautiful new club was in chaos. So the property committee immediately had a shower house built outside the club where victims of shipwreck could be cleaned up before coming inside.

At the next meeting, there was a split in the club membership. Most of the members wanted to stop the club's lifesaving activities as being unpleasant and a hindrance to the normal social life of the club. Some members insisted upon lifesaving as their primary purpose and pointed out that they were still called a lifesaving station. But they were finally voted down and told that if they wanted to save lives of all the various kinds of people who were shipwrecked in those waters, they could begin their own lifesaving station down the coast. They did.

As the years went by, the new station experienced the same changes that had occurred in the old. It evolved into a club, and yet another lifesaving station was founded. History continued to repeat itself, and if you visit that sea coast today, you will find a number of exclusive clubs along that shore. Shipwrecks are frequent in those waters, but most of the people drown.*

CHALLENGE

Do you have the fellowship you need to be a growing Christian? Are you an active coparticipant in your church, or are you a pew-sitter? God loves the church so much that His desire for every believer is to be committed to His church and be active in the fellowship.

---

* *Ideas Books #5-8* (El Cajon: Youth Specialties, 1970), pp. 78-79.

DAY 5

Walking the Fence

I know your deeds, that you are neither cold nor hot. I wish you were either one or the other! So, because you are lukewarm—neither hot nor cold—I am about to spit you out of my mouth.
—Revelation 3:15,16

Everyone at one time or another has tried to keep his balance while walking on a fence. Sometimes we make it and sometimes we fall. When it comes to obedience, far too many Christians try to "walk the fence." They keep one foot in the Spirit while one foot flirts with the world. These are some of the unhappiest people in the world.

Charles Spurgeon once said, "I never saw anybody try to walk on both sides of the street but a drunken man; he tried it, and it was awkward work indeed; but I have seen many people in a moral point of view try to walk on both sides of the street, and I thought there was some kind of intoxication in them."

If God is God and Christ is our Savior, let us

give our undivided attention and whole hearts to God. A lukewarm Christian never has the joy of knowing the fullness of God. Obedience is the key to real faith. This is real faith: believing and acting obediently regardless of circumstances.

CHALLENGE

If there are areas of your life where you are walking the fence, make a decision today to act in obedience and to experience the fullness of God. It will take a single-minded obedience in faith.

DAY 6

Attempting the Impossible

During the fourth watch of the night Jesus went out to them, walking on the lake. When the disciples saw him walking on the lake, they were terrified. "It's a ghost," they said, and cried out in fear.

But Jesus immediately said to them: "Take courage! It is I. Don't be afraid."

"Lord, if it's you," Peter replied, "tell me to come to you on the water."

"Come," he said.

Then Peter got down out of the boat and walked on the water to Jesus. But when he saw the wind, he was afraid and, beginning to sink, cried out, "Lord, save me!"

Immediately Jesus reached out his hand and caught him. "You of little faith," he said, "why did you doubt?"

And when they climbed into the boat, the wind died down. Then those who were in the boat worshiped him, saying, "Truly you are the Son of God."

—Matthew 14:25-33

In this story Peter's lack of faith forced him to sink so that Jesus had to save him, but Peter is to be commended for stepping out of the boat and attempting to walk on the water. You'll notice that the other disciples were not exactly fighting to join Peter! Living by faith sometimes means stepping out into the unknown and depending on God to carry us through.

I'm afraid that too many times I never step out of the boat, and in my comfortable lifestyle I miss out on the fullness of God. People who walk by faith aren't afraid to attempt the impossible. I hope you are a person who places your life in the hands of God and walks on the side of the impossible.

This statement by Dr. Carl Bates reminds me to keep away from the comfortable and attempt something greater than my ability:

> There came a time in my life when I earnestly prayed, "God I want Your power!"
>
> Time wore on and the power did not come.
>
> One day the burden was more than I could bear.
> "God, why haven't You answered that prayer?"
>
> God seemed to whisper back His simple reply,

"With plans no bigger than yours, you
don't need My power."*

CHALLENGE

Are you willing to be included among those who
step out in faith and depend on the power of God?
Peter's walk on water was a life-changing experience for him, and he found that Jesus would be
with him if he started to sink.

---

* Bill Glass, *Expect to Win* (Waco: Word, 1981),
p. 52.

DAY 7

Dare to Dream

I can do everything through him who gives me strength.

—Philippians 4:13

I once heard it said, "I would rather attempt something great and fail than attempt nothing and succeed." What dream is God placing in your heart? Don't sit back and wait for someone else to make a difference when you can be that person. The world doesn't need more armchair quarterbacks; the world needs people like *you* to get in the arena and give it everything you can! It was President Theodore Roosevelt who said:

> It is not the critic who counts; not the man who points out how the strong man stumbled or where the doer of deeds could have done them better. The credit belongs to the man who is actually in the arena; whose face is marred by dust and sweat and blood; who strives valiantly;

who errs, and comes short again and again, because there is no effort without error and shortcoming; who does actually try to do the deed; who knows the great enthusiasm, the great devotion, and spends himself in a worthy cause; who, at the worst, if he fails, at least fails while daring greatly.*

Our Lord plants a dream in everyone's heart. Most often the dreams are mighty, life-changing dreams with long-term positive results. Take your dream, then take the words of Paul, "I can do everything through him who gives me strength," and make a difference in this world!

CHALLENGE

What dream has God planted in your heart? What decisions in your life do you need to make in order to bring that dream to reality? It's time to move on to that dream!

---

* Ted W. Engstrom, *The Pursuit of Excellence* (Grand Rapids: Zondervan, 1982), p. 57.

12 *ENCOURAGEMENT*

DAY 1

Reach Out and Touch Someone

Dear friends, let us love one another, for love comes from God. Everyone who loves has been born of God and knows God. Whoever does not love does not know God, because God is love.
—1 John 4:7,8

I love this story and want to share it with you.

Ever feel like a frog? Frogs feel slow, low, ugly, puffed, drooped, pooped. I know. One told me. The frog feeling comes when you want to be bright but feel dumb, when you want to share but are selfish, when you want to be thankful but feel resentment, when you want to be great but are small, when you want to care but are indifferent.

Yes, at one time or another each of us has found himself on a lily pad floating down the great river of life. Frightened and disgusted, we are too froggish to budge.

Once upon a time there was a frog. But he really wasn't a frog. He was a prince who looked and felt like a frog. A wicked witch had cast a spell on him. Only the kiss of a beautiful maiden could save him. But since when do cute chicks kiss frogs? So there he sat, unkissed prince in frog form. But miracles happen. One day a beautiful maiden grabbed him up and gave him a big smack. Crash! Boom! Zap! There he was, a handsome prince. And you know the rest. They lived happily ever after.*

As a Christian you can be used by God to help change people. Who is the frog in your life who has the potential of becoming a prince or princess? Your touch has the power to begin a change in him or her. I don't think there is anything greater than being one of God's assistants and helping Him in His work of changing human beings. Don't miss the wonderful experience of servanthood!

CHALLENGE

Think of someone who needs your love and attention. Look beyond his flaws and froggish behavior to who he can become in Christ. Take him on as your special project. Don't delay. Your touch may be all he needs!

---

* Wes Seeliger in church bulletin quoted in Bruce Larson, *Ask Me to Dance* (Waco: Word, 1972), pp. 11-12.

DAY 2

Be Liberal with Encouragement

Encourage one another and build each other up, just as in fact you are doing.
—1 Thessalonians 5:11

Mark Twain once said, "I can live two months on one good compliment." People need your praise and affirmation. Be liberal with your gift of encouragement and always be on the lookout for opportunities to lift someone's spirits.

A woman in my church has a ministry of affirmation. She must have stock in the local stationery store, because she is always writing affirming notes. I save those notes, and I've received eight this year! Her willingness to praise someone for a job well done or encourage a person who needs a moment of inspiration has given my friend a profound ministry. She'll probably never give a sermon, write a book, or be famous, but I guarantee you that in God's eyes her notes of encouragement are more powerful than most sermons you've ever heard.

Is there someone in your life who needs a little affirmation and praise? What better gift to give him than the gift of encouragement!

CHALLENGE

Don't wait another day to give encouragement to someone who needs it. Maybe it will come in the form of a note, a phone call, or a freshly baked batch of cookies. He will appreciate it and you'll be a better person for it!

DAY 3

Your Smile Costs Nothing But Gives Much

Dear friends, let us love one another, for love comes from God. Everyone who loves has been born of God and knows God. Whoever does not love does not know God, because God is love.
— 1 John 4:7,8

One of the greatest ways to love someone is to give him your smile. I have long forgotten where I found this profound thought, but I share it with you and challenge you to share your smile with someone else today.

A smile costs nothing, but gives much. It enriches those who receive, without making poorer those who give. It takes but a moment, but the memory of it sometimes lasts forever. None is so rich or mighty that he can get along without it, and none is so poor but that he can be made rich by it. Yet it cannot be bought, begged, borrowed, or stolen, for it is something that is of no value to anyone until it is given away. Some people are too tired to give you a smile. Give them one of yours, as none needs a smile so much as he who has no more to give.

CHALLENGE

God gave you your smile so you could give it away. Sometimes God uses a simple smile to change the life of someone who needs it. Sometimes the first step of sharing your faith is your smile. Who needs your smile today?

The Adjustments of Love

My command is this: Love each other as I have loved you. Greater love has no one than this, that one lay down his life for his friends.

—John 15:12,13

A surgeon wrote this story about an experience that changed his life.

> I stand by the bed where a young woman lies, her face postoperative, her mouth twisted in palsy, clownish. A tiny twig of the facial nerve, the one to the muscles of her mouth, has been severed. She will be thus from now on. The surgeon had followed with religious fervor the curve of her flesh; I promise you that. Nevertheless, to remove the tumor in her cheek, I had cut the little nerve. Her young husband is in the room. He stands on the

213

opposite side of the bed, and together they seem to dwell in the evening lamplight, isolated from me, private. Who are they, I ask myself, he and this wry-mouth I have made, who gaze at and touch each other so generously, greedily? The young woman speaks. "Will my mouth always be like this?" she asks. "Yes," I say, "it will. It is because the nerve was cut." She nods and is silent. But the young man smiles. "I like it," he says. "It is kind of cute." All at once I know who he is. I understand, and lower my gaze. One is not bold in an encounter with a great man. Unmindful, he bends to kiss her crooked mouth, and I am so close I can see how he twists his own lips to accommodate to hers, to show her that their kiss still works.*

This husband was a great man. In the midst of what could have been a horrible experience for all, he rose above his shock: He accommodated his life and kiss to set his wife at ease.

As a Christian you are called to adjust your life to serve your fellow human family. What is God calling you to do with your life? Are you willing to follow His call? Are you willing to make some adjustments to your lifestyle if necessary?

---

* *Parable Newsletter*, January 1983, p. 3.

CHALLENGE

What can you do with your life to make it count?
Is there a part of your life that you've been
complaining about that really would be better off if
you took a different attitude about it? Today make
an accommodation of love that you've needed to
make for a long time. God smiles as a proud
Father, knowing that you are making the right
decision.

*Bulso
9-27-99*

Actions Speak Louder Than Words

Dear children, let us not love with words or tongue but with actions and in truth.

—1 John 3:18

Your actions will speak much louder than any words you will ever say. When you call yourself a Christian you are opening your life up for inspection, and your life becomes an active witness for Jesus Christ. The positive news is that people will respond to your good deeds and thoughtful acts of caring. In fact people will want to know more about the Savior you love, as your deeds prove to them that your faith is more walk than talk.

Here's a story with an important message:

Shortly after World War II came to a close, Europe began picking up the pieces. Much of the Old Country had been ravaged by war and was in ruins.

Perhaps the saddest sight of all was that of little orphaned children starving in the streets of those war-torn cities.

Early one chilly morning an American soldier was making his way back to the barracks in London. As he turned the corner in his jeep, he spotted a little lad with his nose pressed to the window of a pastry shop. Inside the cook was kneading dough for a fresh batch of doughnuts. The hungry boy stared in silence, watching every move. The soldier pulled his jeep to the curb, stopped, got out, and walked quietly over to where the little fellow was standing. Through the steamed-up window he could see the mouth-watering morsels as they were being pulled from the oven, piping hot. The boy salivated and released a slight groan as he watched the cook place them onto the glass-enclosed counter ever so carefully.

The soldier's heart went out to the nameless orphan as he stood beside him.

"Son...would you like some of those?" The boy was startled.

"Oh, yeah...I would!"

The American stepped inside and bought a dozen, put them in a bag, and walked back to where the lad was standing in the foggy cold of the London morning. He smiled, held out the bag, and said simply:

"Here you are."

As he turned to walk away, he felt a tug on his coat. He looked back and heard the child ask quietly:

"Mister...are you God?"

We are never more like God than when we give.

"God so loved the world, that He gave...."*

CHALLENGE

What act of kindness or gift of love can you give to someone today? Is your lifestyle representing Jesus in a positive manner with your deeds?

---

* Charles Swindoll, *Improving Your Serve* (Waco: Word, 1981), pp. 52-53.

DAY 6

Friendship: A
Priceless Gift

A friend loves at all times.

—Proverbs 17:17

There are very few things in life as important or
as wonderful as true friendship. A good friend is a
treasure beyond almost anything else in life.
Friendship is a priceless gift from God.

Iverson Williams once wrote:

Friendship is a special blessing from
above. It's sharing of activities with someone who understands and cares. It's a
warm ray of sunshine that fills our hearts
in times of need. It's bringing out of beautiful things in each other that no one else
looked hard enough to find. It's the
mutual trust and honesty that lets us be
ourselves at all times.

CHALLENGE

Take a moment to thank God for your friends. Seek ways today and this week to be a better friend to other people.

I Stand by the Door

I am the door; if any one enters by me, he will
be saved, and will go in and out and find pasture.
                    —John 10:9 RSV

Sam Shoemaker spent his life helping people find
new life and meaning in Jesus Christ. He had a
special love for those who had never made a commitment to Jesus Christ. One day he sat down to
write his philosophy of life, and he penned this
work of prose.

I stand by the door.
I neither go too far in, nor stay too far
    out.
The door is the most important door in
    the world—
It is the door through which men walk
    when they find God.
There's no use my going way inside, and
    staying there,
When so many are still outside and they,
    as much as I,

Crave to know where the door is.
And all that so many ever find
Is only the wall where a door ought to be.
They creep along the wall like blind men,
With outstretched, groping hands.
Feeling for a door, knowing there must be
    a door,
Yet they never find it...
So I stand by the door.
The most tremendous thing in the world
Is for men to find that door—the door
    to God.*

Do you know someone who needs to be introduced to the new life that Jesus Christ offers? Maybe you are the one to introduce them to your Lord. Since I know that in Christ people can find new life, why am I so shy about introducing them to the *source* of new life? If I really love them, I'll give them the same opportunity to come in the door and meet the Master that I have had. How about you? Is it time to hang around the door and make some introductions?

CHALLENGE

Who do you know who needs to be introduced to Jesus Christ? What's keeping you from helping them meet? Reread Sam Shoemaker's thoughts and then pray for an opportunity to do some introducing!

---

* Helen Smith Shoemaker, *I Stand By The Door* (Waco: Word, 1978), preface.